How to Be More Confident with Women

ENDORSEMENTS

"*Confident with Women* by Dilan Jay is an invaluable guidebook for men when it comes to relating successfully with women. It goes beyond surface tactics and gives actionable, practical tips for men to develop their self-confidence and people skills— skills important in any relationship but especially important when it comes to dating. Dilan goes on to show how to use these essential skills to interact with women on a relational level that invites connection. This simple but profound shift will change your perspective and equip you to create meaning-ful and long-lasting relationships."

—**Susie Miller,** Speaker, Executive Coach,
Author of *Listen, Learn, Love*

"I found the principles in this book to be absolutely profound. They can be applied not only in the dating scene, but in any social environment. The information throughout the pages may be relevant even a century from now, so I'd label this one a perennial."

—Reggie Dissanayake U.S Bank

"*How to Be More Confident with Women* is an honest, modest, and balanced take on that which many struggle to confidently approach: Dating. Where most dating and/or relationship coaches, seminars or tutorials fall short, Dilan Jay truly shines through anecdotes and life lessons that counter the stigma associated with modern dating. Rather than reinforce the ruses or 'special methods' we've all come to know, *How to Be More Confident with Women* urges each of us to dig deeper into what we're looking for in relationships, and, more importantly, why. This all culminates in a light yet intriguing read that is one part story-telling, one part data, and one part common sense."

—Evan Miranda, Greenlight Group

"This book provides sensible advice in the form of a 'How to' created for the guy who is looking for that special lady who is also going to be his BEST FRIEND! Starting with how to have the right attitude, how to know what you want, and how to take the time to get to know the person, this book really does help you start, restart or continue with your search with CONFIDENCE."

—Barry Coziahr, Stampede Branding

"A powerful journey into the world of genuine human interaction and psychology. This book prepares you for the do's and don'ts of forging meaningful connections. A must-read!"

—Omer Ivanir, Triwest

"There are many books at our disposal to learn how to date and build confidence, and most are written in such a way that they leave you filled with even more self-doubt and invalidation. But Dilan is able to turn a lot of our own doubts into strengths that shouldn't be ignored. The other books reinforce your beta male by implementing psychological insecurities rather than increasing your confidence and self-discipline. Dilan actually helps you find the alpha male that's buried inside each of us!"

—Roberto Banke, Banke Global Health

"Finally, a book for guys from a guy that isn't trying to teach you how to just seduce a woman or get her into bed. From a woman's perspective, the advice is spot on. Players beware. This book is not for you. This is for normal guys trying to land a really good girl and be in a normal relationship. What a concept. Good read!"

—Nicole Rodrigues, NRPR Group

"Dilan Jay offers an accessible and effective way to forge meaningful connections in the modern world. His insights inspire a shift in consciousness that will attract a romantic partner and transform your life."

—Autumn Porter, Autumn's SuperNatural Cookies

HOW TO BE MORE CONFIDENT WITH WOMEN

7 EASY STEPS FOR THE GENUINE GUY

DILAN JAY

NEW YORK

LONDON • NASHVILLE • MELBOURNE • VANCOUVER

How to Be More Confident with Women

7 Easy Steps for the Genuine Guy

Published in New York, New York, by Morgan James Publishing. Morgan James is a trademark of Morgan James, LLC. www.MorganJamesPublishing.com

ISBN 9781631953095 paperback
ISBN 9781631953101 eBook
Library of Congress Control Number: 2020945013

Edited by:
Jenn Ryan and Sissi Haner

Interior Design by:
Christopher Kirk
www.GFSstudio.com

Cartoon Design By:
Denzel Erinne

Photography By:
Karine Simon Photography
www.karinesimonphotography.com

Morgan James is a proud partner of Habitat for Humanity Peninsula and Greater Williamsburg. Partners in building since 2006.

Get involved today! Visit
MorganJamesPublishing.com/giving-back

TABLE OF CONTENTS

ACKNOWLEDGMENTS

When it comes to writing the acknowledgments page in a book, it can be perfunctory, and may not convey how the writer *really* feels about the people who helped him along the way. So, let's change that!

Jennifer Anne Thompson, you are amazing, and I LOVE YOU! Thank you so much for helping make this book a reality! Thank you for making me a better writer and a stronger man. Jenn, you helped me take my book and turn it into a BOOK! You are the Don to my Juan, the bun to my burger, the table to my chairs. I have boundless love and respect for you. I want to acknowledge you for all the hard work you did on this book and let you know I could not have done it without you!

I also want to thank **Morgan James Publishing**, and especially **Karen Anderson**, for believing in the book and my vision of giving my fellow man an honest way to act and interact with women—a way that is genuine, real, and always welcomed by women.

Lastly, I want to thank my editor **Sissi Haner** for doing an incredible edit on the book. She kept my voice in the book while still extracting all the important points and making them more visibly notable.

It takes a team to create success for any one man, and this is my team! Thank you to all of you!

AUTHOR'S NOTE

The Elephant in the Room

Before we can even get started, I need to address the elephant in the room: COVID-19. Whether you are reading this book in 2021 or years from now, you probably know that the coronavirus pandemic rocked the world in the worst way possible. Personally, as an entertainer and entrepreneur, this global virus not only destroyed my business, it sunk the very companies that support it (e.g. venues, bars, promotional companies, record labels). Even as I write this in Los Angeles, we live in a "yoyo" reality of one week being allowed to go out in social settings—and then the next week, the governor announces we have to stay at home and avoid people at all costs "for the safety of others." Frustrating!

How do you meet women when disaster strikes?

You will find in this book the basic principles of meeting women, and when I say "basic," I mean that this information's application remains constant no matter what happens in the world at large. As an example, let's take eating. You can travel to 40 different countries and eat 15 different cuisines, but the basic action of eating is, and will always be, putting food into your mouth, chewing, and swallowing. That will never change.

So, I want to assure you in these very interesting times we are in that this book has become even more relevant—not less. *How to Be More Confident with Women* contains the barebones basics of meeting women, which can be applied when you are out with friends (if you get the chance), when you are online, when you are swimming, when you are working out, when you are at home on Instagram, or when you pass a woman on a neighborhood walk while you both are wearing masks.

Ultimately, the modality through which you meet women doesn't matter, but what does matter is exactly what the 7 steps in this book lays out. You are looking for love and companionship. That, too, is basic! You will find how you can discover that in this book!

So, look no further, don't hesitate, read this book! Take these principles I wrote, learn them, and become the confident man you are meant to be! And the next time a pandemic or other local or global disaster strikes? Not only will you be ready, but likely if you follow the steps in this book, you'll already be with a fantastic woman.

INTRODUCTION

L et's start by talking about why I decided to write this book. Not only do I want to shed some light on the do's and don'ts of how to be more confident with women, but I also hope to shift your viewpoint on human interaction. Since this book is about dating, I need to bluntly point out what *not* to do with women, in general, to start us off.

In short, you don't want to be "that dude." And what does it mean to not be "that dude"? It means to not be that stereotypical male misogynist who uses psychology tricks and mind games to get as many women in bed as possible. Everything I see on You-Tube—those "tutorials" for men on how to meet women—is, frankly, weird and calls upon men to "use special methods" to meet women. Let me debunk this misguided idea now.

There are no "special methods" to meet women.

Many of us didn't have a parent, older brother, or good homie who sat down and gave us the real "talk" we needed about women. And I'm not exempt from this! My dad was way too busy working to realize I needed help interacting with girls when I was growing up. If you didn't have that parent or homie in your life who leveled with you on how to meet women, then consider me that homie. And if you did get some guidance in this area, and it never worked for you how you thought it should, keep reading because the 7 steps in this book work.

First, I don't have a Ph.D. in psychology or sociology or any other such field, so I won't bore you with a bunch of theories that don't work in real-life situations. I always think of the "School Spirit Skit 2" off the Kanye West album *The College Dropout* when I read stuff from people who have tons of degrees. He jokes that people accumulate all these degrees and knowledge, but they haven't done anything real in their lives. That's what I think of when I see dating books written by so-called "experts"—sure, the acronyms behind their names look impressive, but have they DONE it?

You need *both* knowledge (theory) and real-life experience. There's a popular adage that people who can't do something, teach it. I don't find this to be true in all instances, but it *is* true when we are talking about meeting women in social settings. I don't care about the person, guy or girl, with a Ph.D. in psychology or marriage and family therapy who spouts all this knowledge about the psychology of meeting women. A college degree is all well and good, but I want to meet the guy who can physically walk into the bar and, within an hour or so, have everybody loving him and wanting to be his friend. You've seen this guy before, I'm sure: girls are digging him, and guys are his new best friends. He's a magnet for people, and this can be you! But you need to learn this way of being with people from someone who not only knows how to do it but has done it himself.

Quick note: The type of information you are about to read in this book can be quite destructive in the wrong hands because bad people tend to find ways to misuse information for their own selfish or deranged purposes. However, the wrong hands wouldn't inherently have the true genuine nature needed to excel in these dating interactions. With that said, I want to clearly state this:

I DON'T CARE FOR PLAYERS.

So, in that sense, I guess I *do* have a Ph.D. ("Player Hating Degree"). Sleeping with large sums of women does nothing for you in the long run. It makes you *less* able to see what is truly right for you and, instead, gets you more focused on a woman's body—not who they are. Not to mention casual, aimless sex becomes quite a distraction and is really time- and attention-consuming. When I was in college, I would have completely disagreed with what I'm saying now, but I also never had anyone give me the honest truth. I made so many mistakes and wasted years of my life. Here's the honest truth: I, just like any other man, am always happier when I am loved and acknowledged.

Love comes from forging meaningful relationships, not one-night stands. So, no matter how cool you may think you are at the time of that one-night stand, you are only hurting yourself, and it will only be you who has to suffer the consequences. Furthermore, it doesn't help a woman when you enable the belief that her value comes from giving a man sex. This couldn't be further from the truth. Minus this mental derailment for both you and her, you need to consider the body points like STDs and unwanted pregnancies, which notoriously come from casual sex. Do yourself a favor and don't be the guy who tries to sleep with tons of women only to—I promise— end up disappointed and alone. Basically, if you're a player and looking for advice on how to trick and sleep with women— THIS BOOK ISN'T FOR YOU.

Meeting women can be described as an art. When done with the right intention in mind, you will be tactful, classy, respected, and successful—not only in your pursuit of women, but in ALL your social interactions that span across friendships, work, and, frankly, the rest of your life. However, walking up to anybody requires confidence, and having confidence is not easy. All the social pressures involved with speaking to women can culminate in man's greatest nightmare: rejection.

Although the information in this book isn't a secret, it definitely wasn't something I knew all my life. In fact, if you were to tell me when I was in middle school that one day I would be writing a book about meeting women, I would have laughed in your face. Back then, I was a scared insecure kid, and I wasn't popular with women, let alone anyone for that matter. I was a scrawny, introverted, pimply, greasy-haired, curry-smelling Sri Lankan kid. Naturally, I didn't just all of sudden jump up out of this situation of being unattractive, horribly awkward, and a grade A weirdo. I had to gradually *learn* how to be confident with women by stumbling upon the answers as I went along in life, and in an effort not to have you reinvent the wheel like I had to, I wrote this book. Thus, I'm happy you've chosen to read this book.

I want you to really understand the concepts I've laid out as I am sure they will help you work through all the insecurities and false information you have inadvertently collected on this subject. This book will change your overall outlook not only on women but people in general, and it will help you tremendously to build your confidence with meeting women, again, without weird gimmicks or games.

I deliberately wrote this book for those nice, genuine, great guys out there who are looking to find their significant other. The 7 steps you're going to read will give you the best chance you have at finding a woman who makes sense for your life *and* future by finding the one who matches you best. The one woman who supports you and truly loves you for *you*, not for what you have or who you are to the outside world.

Remember:

You can do so much more with a partner, especially when it comes to the pursuit of living and enjoying your life.

Humans are social creatures and, without human interaction and real friends, you might find yourself not living your life to its fullest potential. This is ultimately why I wrote this book: to help you find your significant other and live your best life!

Each of the 7 steps are equally as important as the other. This book is meant to be read in sequence *and* in its entirety, so

I strongly recommend not skipping ahead as one idea and step builds upon the next to create an action-oriented and theoretical foundation that will make you more capable and successful with women. This book is for YOU. It's your guidebook to improve yourself socially. This isn't a sales pitch, and this isn't a gimmick. It is real shit from one man to another. It wasn't until I had a long conversation with a friend about meeting women that I realized just how much men needed this information, especially with all the twisted dating information so readily available with just a click of a button.

I'm determined to give you a new, fresh, and workable viewpoint on human interaction, not only with women, but with the world at large. If you understand and apply the 7 steps, you will move through any fears you have speaking to women and/or interacting with others in general. With practice and persistence, you will have no problem meeting women and, eventually, encountering the one you want to build your future with.

So, let's begin, shall we?

THE APPROACH

L et's get right to it: How do you approach a woman? Take a minute or two and review some of your most recent interactions. How did they go? What happened? Where did the interaction fall off the rails (assuming it did)? What you're going to learn in Step 1 may shed some light on what went wrong in previous interactions, so keep reading!

Intention First

Approach is actually a two-part process. Before someone can approach, they have to have an *intention* to approach. That's the first part. You don't just walk up to random people without a reason for approaching them, right? Meaning, on your way to approaching a person, you already have some preconceived notion as to *why* you're setting out to talk to them. It could be as simple as, "damn, she is hot, I want to talk to her" or "he looks like he's watching the game that I want to see" or "he looks like a fun person I should know." So, before we can jump to part two of the Approach—the *physical* approach itself—we need to talk about the first part of the Approach, which is your intention.

The number one mistake men make when they enter a social gathering isn't their approach, as in, what they say, how they go about the communication, what they're wearing, or their body language. The problem is their intention. They want to find a girl to hit on, sleep with, or a girl they think might like them immediately.

This approach = FAIL.

This just-trying-to-find-a-girl thought process is so granular to the bigger picture of what social gatherings are about that you have lost before you even got a chance to start. You've already built yourself a trap. So, you need to understand a lot more about people and being social in order to truly win at approaching a girl.

Let's delve a little bit into the human psyche here at a practical level. What do people want? What do **you** want? You could argue that this answer is significantly different for everyone, right? Well, let's break this concept of what people want down to its bare bones. From the most social guy on the block to the loner hanging out by himself, believe it or not, they have something in common. They both seek out people who understand them. Maybe it is their brother, mother, another loner, whoever it may end up being, the human connection is vital not only for learning about life but for actually *living* life.

If you have ever seen the movie *Castaway* with Tom Hanks, you'll remember how he goes almost nuts living by himself. He pines for human companionship so much so that he takes a beat-up volleyball, draws a face on it, names it "Wilson," and has conversations with it to prevent himself from totally going insane. In other words, people need connection in life so much that, when desperate (or stranded on an island), they'll create it out of nothing (or a volleyball).

What am I getting at here? Just this:

Being understood is the #1 most important thing someone seeks out in life.

Let's take music as another way to illustrate this point. Have you ever noticed that when you go through a break-up, all of a sudden, you relate to sappy, depressing music? Or, if you feel like life is a constant war or struggle, rap music appeals to you? These are types of music that speak to you because you feel like the artist communicates *directly* to you and thus understands you.

Your friends become your friends because you easily understand each other and can see each other's viewpoints. This back and forth understanding of each other makes you inherently feel acknowledged and seen as a person, and it feels satiating, which makes you keep coming back for more and, thus, continue the friendship. Friendships end when you feel unacknowledged, ignored, blown off, misunderstood, or disrespected.

If you doubt that acknowledgment is as powerful as I'm saying, here's a quick way to test my theory. Have you ever been talking to someone and felt like they weren't listening to a word you said? Maybe you came home after a long day and told your roommate, girlfriend, or brother a story about how the day went, and they did not even respond. Isn't that irritating? You immediately got mad or completely disinterested in talking to that person from there on out, right? Why is that? Why can't you just shrug off their ignoring you and not be bothered by it? Simple. They didn't acknowledge you and what you were saying, and that is inherently, at a basic human level, *extremely* frustrating. And lack of acknowledgment will make us turn away from anything—not just relationships, but jobs, dreams, projects, and more. Even the slightest hint of not being acknowledged will cause us to shy away from pursuing new relationships, or social settings at minimum.

A comedian is another great example. What is the purpose of a comedian if he isn't getting others to laugh? I mean, that literally IS the point of being a comedian: making *people* (not walls or houseplants) laugh! Comedians, through their art of funny communication and jokes, actively seek people to understand them and acknowledge their craft through loud, boisterous laughter. Creating art without sharing it is death for an artist. Just look at how many artists drown themselves in drugs and alcohol and prematurely die. It's terrible! Lack of being understood and acknowledged means actual or theoretical death for *anyone* because it makes them feel alienated and utterly alone, no matter how good of a job they're doing.

Let's take a father who works a 9-5 desk job. He drives the awful commute to work every day and begrudgingly toils away because this is what he has to do to put food on the table for his family. His work doesn't receive much notice from anybody, including his boss, and his kids and wife have no idea how much he hates what he does for over 40 hours every week. He's working hard, but with no acknowledgment, and thus he's unhappy, even though he's successful at making an honest living and providing for his family.

Now imagine how happy he would be if he won Employee of the Month at his company, or when he came home, his wife started thanking and praising him for working so hard so his family can live in their beautiful, safe home. In fact, in celebration of his hard work, she cooks him his favorite meal: pot roast with potatoes and cheesecake for dessert. He still has his mind-draining job, but is he a happier more energetic man? Absolutely.

These simple acknowledgements are actually very powerful because they dictate how a man feels his worth. Acknowledgements show a man he is loved, important, and needed. And being shown that you matter validates you and fortifies your strength and confidence in life. Yet, despite how critical acknowledgement and feeling understood are, they can seemingly be hard to obtain. And trust me, I know this from personal experience all too well.

Back when I was in school, it was tough for me to assimilate socially. Trying to be understood when I was one of the only dark-skinned, ethnic people in school was no easy feat because people looked at me as different and, therefore, very unrelatable. I am Sri Lankan by heritage, so people would look at me and not be able to figure out what I was. Was I Mexican? Indian? Black? What was I? I thought college would be different, but even after high school, I experienced this social conundrum. I again felt very left out. All the minority races had grouped up and created clubs. There was an Indian club, Indonesian club, Black club, Chinese club, Latin club, etc. There was no Sri Lankan club! There was no "hey, if you don't belong to any of these clubs join our loners' club." I felt like I didn't have a place in college, even amongst 30,000 students, which made me feel so unacknowledged and unimportant, not to mention lost.

Here's my point. Since this book is about becoming confident with women, if we as guys want to be understood and accepted, we can deduce that women also want to feel understood and accepted. The human psyche isn't different for men and women; we are equal in our ability to think, act, and feel. Thus, we're all in the same boat—we all want to belong and feel understood and included in this game of life.

> **And if you as a man can bring *that* to a woman,
> you're going to win.**

You're Not Alone

Let's take a look at the social landscape today. Since internet dating has become the "normal" way to date, we have this idea that we must show ourselves off so someone will take notice. This idea is false, but because so many people use internet dating, this idea has become insidious. According to a Pew Research Center survey done in 2019[1], 86% of people under the age of 50 have used internet dating. But what most people

---

1 Vogels, Emily A. "10 Facts about Americans and Online Dating." Pew Research Center. Pew Research Center, February 6, 2020. https://www.pewresearch.org/fact-tank/2020/02/06/10-facts-about-americans-and-online-dating/.

don't know is that just 33% of that 86% end up in committed relationships or married. That means every two out of three times someone uses internet dating apps, it does not result in a committed relationship. Those numbers don't make it a successful avenue, again, if your goal is to find a real relationship that enriches your life.

Coupled with the fact that you are basically a needle in a haystack, the way these dating apps are set up, women are bombarded with messages from men who are looking solely at their pictures to evaluate whether this woman is the right person for them. Women who want this kind of attention put more and more sexy pictures up, and men who seek only a body get more and more distracted by looking at just pictures of a body and not the person herself. This leaves the great girls with class with little to no attention and the normal guys completely brain-farted on what they got on the app originally to find. From this perspective, you can see we have gotten way off track as a society when it comes to dating by relying on image-centric apps.

Yet, with the promise of technology to draw us closer together—which in many cases it does—we find ourselves still lonely. And guess what loneliness is a byproduct of? Not feeling acknowledged. In a study by Cigna[2] where 20,000 adults aged 18 and older were surveyed using the UCLA Loneliness Scale, it was found that nearly half of Americans always or sometimes feel alone or left out. In fact, the same Cigna study showed that 56% of people reported feeling like the people

---

2   "New Cigna Study Reveals Loneliness at Epidemic Levels in America." Cigna, a Global Health Insurance and Health Service Company. Cigna Corporation, May 1, 2018. https://www.cigna.com/newsroom/news-releases/2018/new-cigna-study-reveals-loneliness-at-epidemic-levels-in-america.

around them are not necessarily with them—another stark indicator of loneliness, which again, applies to more than half of those surveyed.

I don't think there is a single person who hasn't felt alienated or different from his peers at some point in his life. In fact, referring back to the survey done by Cigna, 1 in 6 adults in the U.S report are suffering from a "mental health condition," and the consistent part of their pathology was they also suffered from loneliness. **Note:** This is just the 20,000 surveyed; likely the percentages could be much more given we spend our lives constantly connected to devices and less out in life meeting people and doing physical activities. Here's what's scary, again from the same study:

"Loneliness has the same impact on mortality as smoking 15 cigarettes a day, making it even more dangerous than obesity."

Plus:

- Generation Z (adults ages 18–22) and Millennials (adults ages 23–37) are lonelier and claim to be in worse health than older generations.
- Social media use alone is not a predictor of loneliness (i.e. using social media more does not prevent or avoid loneliness).
- Students have higher loneliness scores than retirees.
- There was no major difference between men and women and no major difference between races when it came to average loneliness scores.
- And this last point, which I feel is the most important is:
- **Individuals who feel less lonely are more likely to engage in in-person interactions.**

What am I getting at? Despite online dating apps seeming to connect people who otherwise wouldn't get connected, they're not necessarily successful per the statistics. Furthermore, people are straight-up lonely, again, despite social media pervading all of our lives and seemingly making us closer. Yet, like I illustrated above, people still yearn to be acknowledged.

If you strangely feel alone when you go out into social gatherings, know this:

You are definitely not alone. The statistics prove it.

Remember that making connections are valuable and finding the right person or group is important to your overall happiness. But do realize that you will have to make a lot of connections to really find "your people," which takes resilience, time, and the willingness to go out and meet people in all sorts of settings.

You're going to experience a viewpoint shift on the subject of meeting new people, which will be vital to getting you out there and being confident with women. Just remember: No one is above you; we are all human beings who intrinsically want the same thing. When you go out, you should go out to meet people, both men *and* women, be social, and HAVE FUN!

Kill this idea that you "need" to find a girl when you go out! Open up to the room! Look around and see who is there—not just the women you want to meet but ALL the people. Your approach in a social gathering should never be "who am I going to sleep with tonight" but rather, *who am I going to create connections with tonight*. And if you think you don't really care about people or meeting them, then you are also saying *you don't really care about doing the work it takes to meet the right girl.* Listen, just by virtue of being at a bar, you might find yourself meeting people, but like anything truly worth having, it takes real work and a concentrated effort to get the *exact* thing you want.

Let's Sum It Up

Okay, here's what you've learned so far in Step 1:

- The Approach has two parts: intention and the physical approach itself.
- Your intention is the #1 most important thing to meeting people genuinely.
- Men and women want to be acknowledged and understood.
- People generally are lonely, making acknowledgement even more valuable.
- Dating apps seem to connect us, but online interactions do not replace in-person ones.
- If you want to expand your life, you need to meet lots of people (men and women).
- And meeting people and making connections requires skill.

Your goal of going out needs to be making connections and having fun—not some ulterior motive.

Now, enough theory—let's get practical. How are you going to apply and use this information? Let's get to it.

When you enter a bar, instead of thinking "I want to find a girl because I am single," or "how do I talk to this girl," think about who in the bar you can *connect with*. Consider **anyone** in the social gathering, popular or not, hot or not, who might be able to enhance your life, or whose life you might be able to enhance by interacting with them.

I am going to give you a basic, easy-to-apply example on what happens when you're approach is genuine, and there is no ulterior motive.

To Have or Not Have: That Is The Answer

Imagine entering a sports bar. Like most sports bars, it is set up in the classic style with an oval bar in the center of a rustic, dark wooden room. The smell of whiskey and beer permeates the air; wooden wainscoting climbs the sides of the walls, brown tables and chairs are scattered all around, filling in the empty space between the walls and the bar. Just above the eye line, you see several huge flat screens positioned at every angle so you can watch the game and not miss a second of it. As a man who loves basketball, when you meet another guy who also likes the same team, how easy is it for you to talk to this guy? Easy, right? You would turn to this bar mate and say, "How about these Lakers," and he replies, "Yeah, man, they are pretty amazing tonight."

From there, the conversation may expand into talking about the players, the game that is currently on, or what you both are drinking. You don't put much effort into striking up a conversation as you are there watching the game, so a lot of the convo fixes onto what's happening in the game, the Lakers' record, and of course, your favorite players. Although the conversation may have been very surface-level and superficial, the interaction itself was natural, and you probably never thought twice about that very common and effortless interaction.

If you and this fellow basketball lover found more than just basketball in common, then you might have made yourself a new friend—minimally, a new guy to hang out and watch games with, right? Well, *every* interaction should be that easy, including interactions with women. So, why isn't it? Because all of sudden something you understand and are willing **to have or not have** (this conversation with the fellow basketball lover) turns into a **need to have** conversation with a woman. And when talking to a woman, it becomes a scenario you "don't want to mess up." Make sense? Let me explain further.

In this situation with another man at a bar, you approached the conversation casually as a friend in an easy-going manner— you pose no threat to the person you are communicating with. You didn't want anything from him, and he didn't want anything from you. You didn't enter into the conversation with hyped-up, preconceived ideas of what was supposed to happen. You simply walked into the bar, saw your favorite team, sat down, got a drink, and saw someone else watching the same game right next to you and had a random convo. You did not invest your emotions or bank the success of your outing on whatever happened in this casual conversation. You just talked to him, and that was it.

In this first step—the Approach—your intention is to approach *everyone* you meet as a possible new friend, *not* as a potential date, a hot girl, or any other consideration. After you understand that the approach is to create *connections*, then the second thing you have to remember is this:

You have to be willing to NOT have the connection
you are potentially trying to make.

Digging deeper into this concept is the idea of being able to *not* have something. Meaning in order to really *have* something, you also have to be willing and able to *not* have something. Referring back to our example of the bar mate watching basketball: If you turned to him and said, "How about those Lakers?" and he didn't respond, you would have looked back at the TV, forgetting about it almost immediately (and possibly thinking the guy was rude). Why? Because all you were offering was friendly conversation, and if he didn't want to have it, who cares!!

You don't care; neither does he. If this bar mate isn't willing to receive friendly conversation, too bad for him, right? So why don't you care? Because your intention was pure. You didn't want anything from him, so in your mind, there wasn't anything to lose—only friendly conversation to gain. This interaction wasn't clouded by sex, looks, and fear of rejection. It was genuinely just a question: "How about those Lakers?"

This viewpoint can also be applied to internet dating. Treat online dating with the same intention you would treat your fellow bar mate. If a woman doesn't want to reciprocate, it is okay. Stay true to what you are looking for ultimately: a soul mate. This book was written to help you find that. In your online dating profile, you say what is real to you, put up the pictures that best represent you, and let it ride. Don't be so attached to how many women reach back out to you. Women who take internet dating seriously and are genuinely looking for a life partner will go through your profile and read what you write in your bio. This is real. But if they want to play games and are looking for the hottest, fastest guy they can find, don't worry about that. That isn't the game you are playing.

Don't Fear the Friend Zone

Getting back to the approach we were talking about in the bar, someone could say, "But I don't want to end up in the friend zone, I am looking to fall in love." Well, I would say you haven't gotten to that point yet. Your aim here in Step 1 isn't to be a girl's boyfriend principally. It is to have a non-threatening interaction with a girl, where it wouldn't matter if she is into it or not. She, just like the bar mate, is just another person in the bar amongst many others. Someone you were just offering friendly conversation to, and if she doesn't want to have this genuinely, then who cares!!

She is a human being like you, with wants, needs, and dreams, again just like you. This separation between women and men has become very hard to avoid with the advent of so many social media apps solely portraying multiple pictures of women and men. This doesn't help you to have natural interactions with people. I could almost guarantee that you have seen more *pictures* of women than you have seen women in person. This ends up making your in-person interactions skewed and awkward because the social media apps paint a fake picture of reality.

Television is fantasy, and social media is a form of television. I would suggest limiting your social media viewing of women as it starts to paint an unreal picture of what is actually happening in real life. I would also strongly advise you not to look at pornography. For men, porn has become "normal" and because of the internet, easily and frequently available, but viewing porn will never help you in real life because it is make-believe. Real life is real life.

Let's get real here. You don't want a social media girlfriend; you want a real one. Put energy into the things you want: You want a real girl to go to real places and meet real people. But as you do this, keep in mind the intention to be genuine about what you say and who you are.

We will go deeper into transitioning these new connections into a possible love interest as we proceed through these steps. But for now, understand the approach. It starts with the right intention, the pure intention of creating connections for the sake of finding people who understand you and vice-versa—for the sake of enhancing one's life through friendly conversation or vice-versa. With intention in mind, being able to have this connection—or not—becomes so much easier, and all the pressure of talking to anybody melts away.

To finish up this step, I want to cite a book I read by Malcolm Gladwell called *The Tipping Point*[3]. He writes about the "Connector," a guy who meets people just for the joy of meeting people. In the excerpt below, Gladwell unfolds some interesting misnomers about Connectors, referring to a gentleman he met by the name of Horchow, who he has justifiably labeled a Connector.

> When I met him, I became convinced that knowing lots of people was a kind of skill, something that someone might set out to do deliberately and that could be perfected, and that those techniques were central to the fact that he knew everyone. I kept asking Horchow how all of the connections in his life had helped him in the business world, because I thought that the two things had to be linked, but the questions seemed to puzzle him.

3   Gladwell, Malcolm. *The Tipping Point*. Little, Brown, 2014.

It wasn't that his connections hadn't helped him. It was that he didn't think of his people collection as a business strategy. He just thought of it as something he did. It was who he was.

Horchow has an instinctive and natural gift for making social connections. He's not aggressive about it. He's not one of those overly social, back-slapping types whose process of acquiring acquaintances is obvious and self-serving. He's more an observer, with the dry, knowing manner of someone who likes to remain a little bit on the outside. He simply likes people, in a genuine and powerful way, and he finds the patterns of acquaintanceship and interaction in which people arrange themselves to be endlessly fascinating.

Although Gladwell talks about a natural disposition that people have to be one or another type of person, I would argue that we all have a little bit of the Connector inside of us. Find your genuine love for mankind and harness it to meet new people. In time, you'll find a great girl.

Step 2

WATCH AND LEARN

Your first interaction: How does it work? What do you say? Watch and Learn isn't about you watching someone else so you can learn *from* them. It is about you watching and learning *about* those individuals you are getting ready to meet. You are looking for physical and social cues, like someone tapping their fingers on the bar (they might be bored) or constantly looking around the room (not interested in the company in front of them). When you enter a bar, work party, school dance, college party, or club, your first job is to look around you—this time, at specific people who grab your attention—both men *and* women.

You are out to enjoy yourself, but if you want to meet people, you will have to adapt a more *pan-determined* approach. What do I mean by pan-determined? Well, according to Merriam-Webster[4], the definition of self-determined is a doctrine in which the actions of self are determined by itself. The prefix *pan*, by definition, means involving all of a (specified) group or region. So, pan-determined simply means being determined for the whole group. The actions of the group and outcome of the group get determined by its group members, which means you play a role in the group every time you are out in a group environment. This is an excellent approach for life as it drives you to find answers for everyone and do the right thing not only for you, but for everyone.

With this pan-determined approach, you will have to be interested in others, what they are doing, and how they are doing it. Being interested in others might seem foreign at first (e.g. caring about the random dude getting drunk in the corner of a bar) because he seemingly has nothing to do with you. Yes, on the surface he doesn't, but we are all connected, and being conscious of that helps to raise your responsibility not only for your fellow man, but Mother Earth.

Let's take this random guy getting drunk by himself. You don't have anything to do with him, per se. But let's say you went and talked to him and found out he was having a really bad day. "XYZ" was pushing him to drink to the point of being belligerent. You find out he was supposed to drive home and, instead, you help him get an Uber. There is no telling

---

4   "Self-determined." Merriam-Webster.com Dictionary, Merriam-Webster, https://www.merriam-webster.com/dictionary/self-determined. Accessed 28 Apr. 2020.

what life you saved by making sure a drunk driver didn't get on the road.

Furthermore, by helping him not drive drunk and thus possibly saving his life, you alleviated untold pain to his loved ones who would've been devastated had he died that night. Plus, there are infinite other adverse outcomes you prevented, again, by helping some random guy grab an Uber. In short, the power you can effect by connecting with random people has infinite outcomes and, not only that, it's based on scientific theory—the Chaos Theory[5].

In the early twentieth century, Edward Norton Lorenz discovered a branch of mathematics that he called the Chaos Theory. To keep it simple, the Chaos Theory states that within the apparent randomness of chaotic, complex systems (life being a great example!), underlying patterns, interconnectedness, repetition, and self-organization exist.

From the Chaos Theory came another theory you've probably heard of: *The butterfly effect*[6]. The butterfly effect describes how a small change in one place can ripple out and effect change in another (different) area or a similar area of the same system. What you do, whether you like it or not per the butterfly effect, has an effect on everything around you and even the world at large. Am I saying that waving your arm in Texas can cause a tornado in South Africa? No. But in terms of amplifying YOUR impact on the world around you, I'm sure you can agree that

5   Bishop, Robert, "Chaos", The Stanford Encyclopedia of Philosophy (Spring 2017 Edition), Edward N. Zalta (ed.), https://plato.stanford.edu/archives/spr2017/entries/chaos/.

6   Vernon, Jamie L. "Understanding the Butterfly Effect." American Scientist, June 12, 2017. https://www.americanscientist.org/article/understanding-the-butterfly-effect.

your actions not only help mold your life but also can mold the lives of others, including those you haven't met.

So, here's my point: When you're in a social gathering, know that you have to be pan-determined for the group. Find the people out there who want to make conversation and find a way to make yourself available to them. Always think you should leave a place in a better condition than when you arrived there, whether by friendly conversation or even throwing away stray trash or straightening your chair when you leave.

When you become interested in others within a social gathering, you will find some very observable types of people. To be clear, I did not dream up this information after watching YouTube videos or even reading books. I've aggregated these insights from many years of meeting people across the globe, giving me a unique backstory from which to write this book.

How It Started

First of all, I have been DJing since I was just 12 years old. For a DJ, the telling sign that he or she is bad at their job is an empty dance floor. So, at a very young age, I looked at people and analyzed them from afar every time I played a song to see whether I was going down the right road of style of music. I looked to see if there was an extra hip in their step, or a happy smile from a song, or someone mouthing the words. These indicators gave me clues so I could navigate the music in the right direction. Thus, I have spent thousands of hours watching other people in social settings, interested because my job and income depended on my ability to observe and react accordingly. I've DJed hundreds of parties, so I have had a definite advantage when it comes to noticing people.

This experience enabled me to aggregate the necessary skills at a very young age, and for so many years the information you're reading has become ingrained in my mind, like a sixth sense. In his book *Outliers*[7], Malcolm Gladwell talks about how spending 10,000 hours practicing or working at anything will make you a professional. Well, I can honestly say I've accumulated 10,000 hours of observing people.

At first as a DJ, I was doing friends' and family parties. Then my brother let me DJ one of his college fraternity parties. And that party led to another gig at a club. Then I met the club promoter who hired me to DJ at their club. Before I knew it, I was DJing all around Los Angeles, and I was only 17. From there, the venues got bigger, and by the time I was 21, I had played for thousands of people. After I graduated from college, I became a producer and singer, and I played for crowds around the world for another 10 years.

My brother and I loved to travel, so we traveled to over 35 countries, exploring the culture of the different countries where we would go to local restaurants, bars, and clubs to meet the locals. I'm sure you can imagine that, mixed into all of this, we met our fair share of women. Since I entered the party scene at age 12, I naturally grew to love and be comfortable in social settings. In fact, most recently, I played at over 100 bars in the past year alone, showcasing my new album.

Amongst these years of traveling and exploring thousands of bars, clubs, restaurants, and event venues, I started to notice the same types of people over and over again in social settings.

---

7   Gladwell, Malcolm. *Outliers: The Story of Success.* New York: Back Bay Books/ Little, Brown, 2009.

Because the sample size was so huge (I couldn't even guess how many people I've met in all those years), I knew when I was seeing outliers in a group scenario, and I cut them out of my evaluation of the three types of people I kept seeing over and over again. Those are the Loners, Stragglers, and Groupers.

The **Loners** are the guys/girls at the bar who don't know anybody and don't necessarily have the gumption to try to meet anybody. Usually, unless someone comes to sit by them accidentally to order a drink or sit down and strike up a convo, they don't really talk to anyone. Imagine that guy who comes to the bar every day. He is there sitting on a lonely stool and orders a drink just to wind down from his workday. He drinks and he thinks. He drinks and he thinks. He has one or two lines of convo with the bartender who knows him quite well, but he is really there for some alone time.

The **Stragglers** are the people who show up with a group but are actually looking to meet new people. They aren't necessarily the life of the party and may appear to trail behind the group, not because they are slow or lazy, but because their ultimate goal is to meet new people, and this is how they hope to do it.

The **Groupers** are the people who appear to be completely satisfied to not talk to anyone else except the people they came with. They're just there to converse with their own group members. Most of the time you see this with women. They come in groups of three or four and sit around and drink together, never really concerning themselves with the outside environment. Typically, when someone does try to break up this party, they are met with off-putting remarks or just made to feel unwanted.

So, just by nature of entering a bar or other social setting, you too will be one of these "types" of people. Do you know which one is you? If you didn't come by yourself, you definitely are not a Loner. A Loner by definition came by himself. If you came with friends with the intention of meeting others, then by definition you are a Straggler. If you came for a friend's party and have no concern about the world around you but to be at your friend's party, you are most likely a Grouper that night. You can be any one of these three types on any given night. You could also have come with a friend who wants to meet other people, so by definition the *both* of you are Stragglers. There isn't just one Straggler in a group, BUT **every group has a Straggler**. I will explain this further below.

Let's go over the three scenarios and how you would interact depending on which type of person you are. First, I want to give you a general modus operandi when you enter a bar, no matter if you have entered as a Loner or Straggler.

When you enter a bar, make sure to "do a lap." Most men do a lap to look at all the hot girls at the bar. I am not asking you to "do a lap" for that reason. I am asking you to do this so you can see the people in your environment and better understand who is there and what group people might fall into. After you've looked around the bar and you've identified the Loners, Stragglers, and Groupers, find out who you actually want to talk to—girl or guy, in a group or not. Find people who look nice and fun to talk to—people you can tell came out to meet people and/or have a good time. This helps you to build your confidence by talking to people in general and builds your confidence for talking to women in the long run. You might be thinking, *well those aren't the people I want to meet. I want to meet the group with all the hot girls.* Yes, but check your intention (Step 1) and go with what makes sense. Remember what you are actually looking for: people of similar ideas and ideals, so you can build long-lasting friendships and relationships. And who knows... one of those "hot girls" may be the one for you. Trust me, it will happen just as long as you stay true to yourself and the goal as mentioned in Step 1.

Loner to Loner

Now here is how the approach would go with Loner to Loner.

If it is a loner, they won't be too difficult to approach as they are already hanging out by themselves, and most of the time they welcome conversation (at least some small talk). However, once again, you have to watch the Loner a little to see what they are drinking, wearing, how they are sitting (are they sitting slouched and depressed, are they waiting for a friend?). You **do** really have to watch.

Once you have identified something they are doing or you are able to figure out what could possibly be on their mind, you can approach this Loner with that thought in mind. What you say should not be too forced. Most of the time a "Hi, I'm (your name), nice to meet you" works almost 85% of the time.

It is really after the initial introduction when the conversation can become silent and awkward. That's why Watch and Learn is important. If you were watching the individual, you'd pick up some cues and, thus, have some ammo to fuel the conversation so you're not just standing there with nothing to say. For instance, if the person is visibly waiting for a friend, after introducing yourself, you could ask, "Are you waiting for your friends?" or something like, "Don't you hate when people are late?" It is typically the first minute of conversation after your introduction that requires a smooth entry, and then from there it's deciding whether to keeping talking to this person or not.

If the person is looking kind of depressed or down, the best way to enter the conversation is with a compliment. Tell them you like something about them (for a woman, you love her shoes)—keep it light and upbeat. If the person looks like they don't want to be disturbed, but you still want to talk to them, you can ask them what they are drinking and if they like it. You would be surprised how many people actually want to talk to someone who they feel is just talking to be social.

Another thing I have found that works really well is before you even make your introduction, you can ask a question or give a compliment. So, if you were to walk up to a person and ask a question like "What you drinking?" or say, "I love that shirt," then people who want to talk will acknowledge you and usually add something to the conversation like, "Thanks, got it from Target" or in the case of the drink, "Yes, it's good, it's a Moscow Mule."

For the Target comment, your response would be something like "I freaking love that store!" or for the drink comment your response would be something like "Did you know they make Moscow Mules with whiskey now?" or if you didn't know that, it could be "What's in a Moscow Mule?" You must say what is most natural to you and non-evaluative to the person you are talking to. The more you can acknowledge, understand, and uplift a person the better.

This is why you must be your most genuine self for these convos because they flow a lot smoother when the real you is there, present and ready to be involved.

An example of something NOT to say to the Target remark would be, "That's such a shitty store" or to the drink, "I hate that drink." This would be an indirect hit on that person's way of life or belief system, and that isn't what you are supposed to be doing when you are out trying to enhance or create new friendships. Everyone has the right to their opinions and/or ideas. If that doesn't work for you, keep it to yourself and keep it moving on to the next interaction. Here is a drawing of what we just spoke about to clarify.

Now let's talk about people in groups and how you would approach them. Since Stragglers are technically part of a group, we will talk about approaching both Stragglers and Groupers together.

The group seems unapproachable, right? But if you are paying attention, you will notice that every group has a Straggler. I'll repeat: Every group has a Straggler. It is this person you want to meet first. Remember, most of the time girls and guys go out together. It is pretty rare that it will be a group of only guys or only girls.

Note: Just like in the hierarchy of the animal kingdom, the male protects the females—even if they are just friends—so never be afraid to meet the guys in the group **first**. It is, in fact, the best way to meet the girls in the group. If you are introduced by a guy friend of a girl, it is almost like the guy announcing to the girls, "It's okay, I like him. He's cool. You should talk to him."

Stragglers are the key to meeting people inside of what would otherwise be a closed group. This brings us to the next way you may have entered a social gathering. If you were not by yourself, you are by default a group member. Thus, if you are looking to meet people outside of your group—which is what we are teaching here in this book—then by nature YOU are the Straggler in the group.

Straggler to Loner

Now here's how the approach would go Straggler to Loner.

A Straggler meeting a Loner is always easy because you (as the Straggler) have the power of your group behind you. You have the power to invite this Loner into your group using your group as leverage. All the same rules of introduction work the same way as Loner to Loner, but you can invite this Loner to hang out with your group, which is a great way to make a friend.

Straggler to Straggler

Now here is how the approach would go Straggler to Straggler.

First, remember, all the introduction points and sentences mentioned in the Loner to Loner section above still apply here, but we again have a couple more options.

When you are meeting a fellow Straggler, you also have the power of using your group as leverage to introduce this Straggler to your group. Remember: *Always introduce your new friend to your group first.* It is a show of good faith, and because we all know the adage *treat others how you would like to be treated*, you will find at this juncture that he or she will feel obliged to introduce you to his or her group. The fellow Straggler you meet may not introduce you to his/her group at that moment, but you have opened the door to allow for the invite.

Also, with Straggler to Straggler, you have a couple more ways to enter this convo: "Are you guys having a birthday party?" or "What's the occasion?" It is quite easy if it is an actual birthday party/occasion as the convo flows. However, if the answer is "just out with friends" and you feel as if you are getting stuck for more convo, remember they are really saying, "just out with friends *to meet new people*," which is especially true for the Straggler you just met. So, you could segue that to say, "Yeah, there are a couple of great bars around here" and give some bars in your local area you like that are great for outings with friends. This will usually open the conversation up to more convo, because they too are looking for cool places and environments.

You have now seen the ways in which to open up a conversation with a random person and have gotten an idea of what makes sense for opener lines. They aren't "hey, you're hot!" or "let me get your number" or "what's your name?" Although this *is* a valid question, I wouldn't recommend it as an opener question.

You'll also notice you will meet a lot more guys at first, and this is okay. Now, I probably meet about the same amount guys and girls, but at first I would always meet guys as they are more approachable, and I have found it easier to have a conversation. But once you start seeing that conversation doesn't change whether you meet a guy or a girl, you won't see the difference between the two in terms of having a friendly, non-threatening conversation!

So, by watching and learning, you will be able to identify the type of people in group settings as well as the most open people to speak to initially. Take your time when you are figuring these things out, but don't overthink it. Use your intuition; it is your greatest gift! Also, remember this is one of many interactions you will be having that evening. So, roll the dice and let it ride! You are there, after all, to have a good time, so don't ever get bogged down on one interaction.

Step 1, the Approach, is mainly about intention. Step 2, Watch and Learn, is about both your environment and the people in it. This step includes pinpointing Loners, Stragglers, and Groupers—giving you the knowledge of how to move to the next step. And only after you know how to move to that next step can you be social with the people in your environment in a non-threatening way.

At this point, you have accomplished what I would call the "first interaction." Let's get on to what happens next!

Step 3

TOUCH AND GO

S tep 3 is the pinnacle to your success with people, as it will garner so much more interest from others in you. What does it mean to "touch and go"? Believe it or not, by now you have already done half of this step! It's quite easy once you have finished setting your intention straight (Step 1) and you've finished your initial interaction (Step 2), which I would consider your "touch." Now, your next move is to walk away: "Go."

Let's make this step clearer by giving you an example so you don't misunderstand it. Suspense movies are notorious for giving you pieces of information that make you wonder what will happen next. You are literally sitting on the edge of your seat because you are wondering what the next move could possibly be.

Say you're watching a murder mystery and, in the beginning, the lights cut out. You hear screams and when the lights turn back on, someone has been murdered. There are five people in the vicinity of where the murder is discovered, and the camera cuts to who you think might be the most obvious murderer. But then it cuts to another person picking up something from the floor looking very guilty, while the next person is coming out of the bathroom still drying his hands. Only five people in the room, but no one has fessed up. You have some small amount of background information on the characters, but you don't know who the murderer is. You're hooked to the screen now and very curious how all this took place in the first 10 minutes of the film! Well, you want to emulate this same sensation of suspense in a social setting—but don't scare the girl LOL.

You should always leave something to be talked about at a later moment, whenever that moment is. Too often I meet someone, and they go on and on about themselves, or tell me so much information about themselves that it is almost hard for me to understand it all. It's noisy in a bar, either with music and/or people. A situation where someone keeps talking and talking only causes me to get disinterested or apathetic toward the person because I am trying to find reasons to get away out from under their barrage of communication.

Here's the secret of making women interested in you immediately:

**Keep the conversation to a minimum
and leave a little bit of mystery.**

Just like in the great suspense thriller, if what happens at the end is revealed at the beginning of the movie, no one will watch the rest of the movie because they already know the end. In other words, people inherently love a little bit of game! A little bit of mystery and a little bit of chase. This is critical to know about people (and life).

When I used to work as a manager for a commercial real estate property, I came across some very unique types of personalities when it came to negotiations. I learned that everyone wants to feel like they got a great deal, so just like most retail stores, I would promote "specials." These "specials" drew people in because it gave them a sense of mystery and being in a game where they can get a better deal than the next guy, or they can get something for cheap. We humans find things, including people, interesting to the degree that there is a bit of challenge in them. If something is 100% predictable and known about from the beginning, it seems boring, so we want it less.

Boredom ruins a lot of great things, because somehow the game has left it. When a job has all of your interest in the beginning but soon becomes "just a job," it's no longer a game; it's now just a boring obligation. Or when you first meet a girl and everything is great in the beginning, and now you have been dating for two years and it's the same rigamarole, there's no variety—everything is known. The game died.

I've seen huge artists make it to the top and then their lives turn into a living hell with drugs and scandals. On the way up, they are shooting for this goal (playing an exciting game) to be the best and win all the awards. Then, once they have it all and they've met their goal, that game is over. Drugs, alcohol, and bad relationships become the new (and distorted) game. People with no problems make problems because they want more activity and challenge where they perceive there is none. This is the reason a majority of privileged kids don't amount to the same greatness as their parents. No challenge, no game.

> *"If you want something done, ask a busy person to do it.*
> *The more things you do, the more things you can do."*
> —Lucille Ball

This busy person plays the game of life and enjoys it.

Free Doesn't Equal Value

Here is an excellent example of when someone is given something for free. Outside clubs and bars, you usually see tons of flyers. People sometimes stand outside of bars and clubs and hand them out. I know this because I used to do it myself by the hundreds every weekend. That's right; I was that guy handing out flyers at the end of the night for my friend's record label in college. And you know where 90% of those flyers ended up? On the floor! People received the flyers for free, so they didn't really care about them. Most of the time, when someone gets something for free, they intuitively feel it's not worth anything, so that's how they treat it. Once again, there is no game involved in getting this flyer, so it's valueless.

How about free ideas? Let's use the example of your parents. When you were growing up, your parents or mentor probably gave you some sage advice that could have easily gotten you out of trouble or kept you safe, but did you take that advice? No.

That advice was too easily accessible and was definitely free, so its value wasn't high to you at all. As teenagers, most of us probably went to the party that got busted by the cops. Or smoked that joint that made us eat two boxes of pizza. Or befriended that surly girl who distracted us from schoolwork and made our grades sink. But how many of us will pay for a book from a spiritual teacher, psychic, doctor, or healer and realize we got the same advice given to us by our mom or dad? Simple advice like "you need to relax" or "don't take it that seriously." So, you can see too much free advice loses its value.

Don't tell your life story when you first meet someone. A woman/man who you just met doesn't care about your autobiography, and the more you verbally vomit on top of them in this first interaction, the lower and lower your value goes. Don't show all your cards right away; create a mystery and make a game, and you'll elicit interest and excitement from a girl, or anyone for that matter!

Remember, though, this concept applies to when you **first** meet someone and are having an **initial** conversation. Knowing to not talk and talk and talk will inevitably help take the pressure off this first interaction when you know inherently that this interaction should be short. Plus, if you keep it short, there will more likely be more than one, which is the point.

You might be thinking, "But if I don't hang on to this girl, some other guy might swoop in and get to be with her or get her number." Yes, this is true, but you are not there for frivolous hook-ups, nor are you in competition with other guys for girls. If she is about hook-ups and finds someone to do that with, that's ultimately the right thing to have happened. If you are looking for a life partner or a girlfriend, but the girl you think could be that is looking to hook up, then you two aren't on the same page and not meant to be together—at least this night. Know your intentions and your values. Remember, you are there to enjoy and to meet multiple people, not just ONE GIRL.

Putting It to Work

Okay, practical lessons now. How does "touch and go" work? You meet a guy at the bar, he asks, "What are you doing here?" You tell him you're "hanging out with some friends for a birthday party." You ask his name, and he asks yours. A silent pause happens. You will feel it. Simply say, "Nice to meet you!" and shake his hand (if appropriate) and go. Great answer; great interaction!

Here is an example of a bad answer.

You say "hi" to someone and they reciprocate, and then you do one of these:

"Well, it's a funny story… we had initially come just to hang out and then my friend randomly sprung on me it was his birthday, and I totally forgot and I feel super bad about it… anyway, though it was supposed to be a birthday party, it doesn't feel like one because I couldn't get a ride here, as I totally wanted to drink and my friend (whose birthday it is) is already drunk, and we all don't have a ride home. So, we are going to Uber, but now we all have to take different Ubers and I have to leave my car here. You think I'll get a ticket?…"

HUH?? DON'T BE THAT GUY! You have given up so much information that it becomes overwhelming, leaving nothing to the imagination for later on. Now, I'm not saying this whole conversation can't be had; I'm saying don't do it in your initial interaction.

Just like in Step 1, you have to be able to *not* have something in order to really have it. Here you have to understand that not all conversation is good conversation, and the ability to *not* say something is just as powerful as the ability to say something. There is power in being neutral and slightly detached. The Buddha taught this often in his lectures. William Shakespeare

once wrote "To be, or not to be, that is the question." I would say a more powerful state of being is to be at peace at being or not being. That is true peace.

The Power of Thought

You ever notice that sometimes when you just think of something or someone, they show up? It's like magic. Right! That is pure thought with no consideration. But other times, when you belabor a thought about wanting a job or woman, you can't ever seem to get to the goal? Yes! This is thought with added consideration. Everything around us is resonating at a frequency. When the frequency nears infinity, you can say it is either so thin or so gargantuan that it can pierce through anything. Your ability to not have something has more to do with not bringing this near infinity frequency of thought down to a more rigid frequency.

The National Research Nuclear University writes[8], "the human body can generate mechanical vibrations at very low frequencies, so-called infrasonic waves. Such low-frequency vibrations are produced by physiological processes—heartbeats, respiratory movements, blood flow in vessels, and other processes. Different organs of the human body produce different resonance frequencies. The heart resonance frequency is about 1 hz. The brain has a resonance frequency of about 10 hz, blood circulation about 0.05 to 0.3 hz."

Extensive research on thought has also been done showing how thought affects the universe at large. Without delving too deeply into a completely different science, it would suffice to say that when you really want something, then the frequency of that thing you want has to be close to infinity. A pure thought with no consideration. When I say, "To have it, you have to be able to not have it," it doesn't mean you're flippant about it either. Someone saying, "I don't care about" or "screw that." That is definitely thought with added consideration. Moreover, it is also not true. You do care and you do want to "screw that" (I'm being

8   Scientists research effects of infrasonic vibrations in humans, October 12, 2016, by National Research Nuclear University, https://phys.org/news/2016-10-scientists-effects-infrasonic-vibrations-humans.html

facetious). It's about knowing that with or without that "thought, idea or desire," you are still great!

There's been so many times in my life, whether it was meeting someone out or even in negotiation, where the person across from me was saying way more than they should have, giving me so much more information than I needed or wanted. Plus, sometimes over-giving information gets you into trouble.

In fact, "the first one to talk loses" concept cited in multiple negotiation books is true. It is not exactly the same in a social setting when you are out with friends, but I'm sure you feel it in your bones when to walk away. However, when you went against your better judgment, hung around for a little too long, it got awkward, and you crashed and burned.

Well, you were right! Let's take the saying "the first one to talk loses" and flip it to read "the first one to shut up wins" and it would do the trick here. There is the magic of timing, but once again, follow your gut here. When it feels like it's time to be quiet, do it! Say, "Nice to meet you," and leave!

Here is an example of reaching just enough in order to leave a mystery. Let's say you meet a girl who is a Straggler (you remember what a Straggler is from the previous step) who is now at the bar. You approach her and say, "I love your shoes!" She turns to you and thanks you. So, you are now ordering a drink (otherwise you shouldn't be at the bar as it would be unnatural), and you are standing right next to this girl. Honestly, from here the comment, "I love your shoes," could be enough. You can withdraw from there and go away. But if you really feel the need to say more, you could possibly say something like, "Not sure if you are a vodka person, but you should try the martinis here; they are really good!" Or you can go as far as introducing yourself to said girl. "My name is (your name), nice to meet you." She would oblige and say the same back. You could also even ask her what she is drinking. But from this point, it's time to move on because that is enough! You made your initial interaction ("touch") and now you need to withdraw from there: "Go."

> **Note:** Stay away from obvious questions like, "What are you doing here? What's your name?" (You should always introduce yourself first).

Remember that awkward feeling after meeting someone where you just don't know what to say? Well, if you start getting it, duck out; you have been there too long. Nobody likes a hanger-on, especially when you have first met them. Imagine you meet a guy in the bathroom when you are at a bar. You are heading back where you and your friends are talking about some girl you like and this dude you met in the bathroom rolls up and pulls himself a seat. AWKWARD!

It is awkward and off-putting. So, in the example of the Loner you met in the previous step, after the compliment and the small talk and introducing yourself, cut out of there and go somewhere else. If you are with friends, go back to your friends. Remember, though, it is always important to get peoples' names. So, when you do happen to go back to see this person again, you now have their name.

Remembering Names

People have this tendency of habitually not remembering people's names. It's almost as if people think it's "cool" to not remember someone's name, as if they know so many people that remembering your name is too hard. If this is you, you should take another look at this behavior/idea. Names are literally how people identify themselves. It is disrespectful and pretentious to not remember people's names. It's like saying, "I am so important and know so many people that remembering your name is too insignificant."

Don't get into this very bad habit. Names are important, and they are extremely helpful when interacting with people (especially strangers) within a public setting. In fact, Dale Carnegie, author of *How to Win Friends and Influence People*[9], wrote, "Remember that a person's name is to that person the sweetest and most important sound in any language. Using a person's name is crucial, especially when meeting those we don't see very often. Respect and acceptance stem from simple acts, such as remembering a person's name and using it whenever appropriate."

Names are important.

---

9   Carnegie, Dale. *How to Win Friends and Influence People*. Pocket Books, 1998.

So, in the case of the Straggler you met and introduced yourself to, when you are by yourself, after you have introduced yourself and he is getting ready to go back to his group, wish him good-bye and be on your way.

If you can "touch and go" two to three times in a night, you will find that by the third time you have created a very real familiarity in a social setting. But don't just take my word for it, because there is a rule of three that has been very well documented.

Three is a magic number. In engineering, the strongest shape is a triangle; in film, we use the three-act sequence; in comedy, punch lines are delivered on the third go-round; and in music, we use the triad to create a chord. Even in nature, the most essential substance on earth, water, is made of two parts hydrogen and one part oxygen (H_2O).

The reason for this is that it takes three to make a pattern, and we humans think in terms of patterns. This is how we have learned to process information. That's why I feel it is important to try to get around to that third time when you are at a social gathering. Don't sell yourself short on the importance of touch and go multiple times in one night.

The first go-round with a girl you meet at the bar is a more instinctive interaction where you are gauging interest and likeness. The second time you will feel more comfortable and speak more freely and have something to talk about (which would be whatever you spoke about earlier), but the third time you will find a very real and natural conversation develop. **A friendship.** Imagine that you are generating touches to go from neutral to aware, from aware to familiar, from familiar to warm, and from warm to HOT, aka, "let's hang out."

This is where you can check your intention and see if you really came out to enjoy the company of others or if you are still out for only yourself. Remember, "to give" will always be more important than "to take." In Sri Lankan culture, this is very much an innate concept. Before we even know your name, we will invite you into our house and feed you a meal. I feel this concept of giving has been lost in time amongst new generations, especially here in America. Due to technology, we have inherently become more introverted, so by merely reaching out to others with genuine hospitality, you'll stand out. Check your ego at the door and remember your purpose of finding real people to interact with and how you could serve the group, not how the group could serve you.

In a bar setting, it is imperative to get around and meet people, and the more people you meet in the beginning, the faster you will find yourself getting into the third round with people.

I am going to diagram out here kind of what it looks like in a typical bar and how this might really work in real world examples.

So, remember Touch and Go. You buy a girl a drink; after you buy it, cut out of there. She most likely is expecting you to talk to her, but unless you really feel it necessary, politely excuse yourself and come back later. **Remember, this isn't about losing anything**. You have to be willing to not have all those things you want so badly. Get used to letting it go from the start, and if in the case you really lose it, it will never hurt that bad.

Drink Users

There is something you should be wary about in bar situations and that is the girl, or group of

girls, called drink users, which has become more and more prevalent in recent years. I have seen it time and time again where you are talking to a girl, or a group of girls, and they keep mentioning how thirsty they are or ask if you are drinking. At first, I would think, "Oh, they want a drink," so I would, of course, offer. I have never been the type to not buy a drink for a fellow bar mate and not think twice about it until I ran into these special users. They are only looking to use an unsuspecting male to buy them drinks. And 95% of the time, it is a girl or group of girls. If you ever run into this, run! They are users and use their beauty and social cues like touching your back or shoulder to make you feel some sort of way to get you to buy drinks for them and their friends… and then they turn around and walk the other way. It's very disheartening to see this.

I hope you don't have this experience. I definitely have had it, so I would like to warn you. Conversely, all the guys who are trying to get women drunk by servicing them with alcohol every time they want it or providing a bottle purely for the idea of getting women drunk to sleep with them, run from them as well. Bad energy only begets bad energy.

Step 4

THE HIERARCHY (POWER IN NUMBERS)

Typically, as a man, you are the initiator. You go out to meet people, you say hi to everyone, you introduce yourself first. The flow is always outward: You do, you act, you talk, you smile. When you learn the hierarchy and how to use your power in numbers, you will be able to flip that flow, bringing people to you!

Have you ever gone to a restaurant or function and noticed one table of people attracting a lot of attention? It looks like all the patrons in the restaurant know them, and those who don't know them already want to get to know them. How does this work? Easy! These people are partying in a large group, and because it's large, they are loud, and by being loud, they are attracting attention. This is an example of a hierarchy in a social setting. In a bar, it could be a birthday party; in school, it's the cool kids; in a club, it's usually the promoter table.

Promoter Tables

> Just in case you aren't savvy on the term promoter table… Night clubs hire promoters whose job is to basically make calls and invite a ton of people they know (in Hollywood they invite mostly girls). So, in exchange for bringing a ton of girls, the bar sets them up with a table and usually one or two bottles of alcohol. In a club, this is usually where a disproportionate amount of girls can be found and where a lot of "hot" girls are.

Your group comprises your hierarchy. A hierarchy is a system or organization in which people or groups are ranked one above the other according to status or authority[10]. The higher up on this hierarchy you go, the more that energetic and communicative flow goes from outward to inward. Let me explain. When you're the top dog in a hierarchy, you're doing your own thing, while others are constantly trying to appeal to you. But the lower you are on the totem pole per se, the more you need to communicate outwardly in order to generate any opportunity or move-

---

10 "Hierarchy." *Merriam-Webster.com Dictionary*, Merriam-Webster, https://www.merriam-webster.com/dictionary/hierarchy. Accessed 29 Apr. 2020.

ment. So, top of the hierarchy, you operate more inwardly, more internally. Lower in the hierarchy, you're operating outwardly to generate more opportunities.

Because most people relate hierarchy to "status," they tend to believe rich people are at the top of the hierarchy, but that's not true when it comes to a social gathering.

Let's take the guy wearing a fancy watch, dressed in expensive clothes. At first glance, you may assume he's the cool guy because he's rich, and therefore you deduce he must be doing something right. Does that make him cool? Does that make him the guy everyone wants to be around? Actually, no. Let me explain.

Now take this same well-dressed guy and put him up against an average guy, your regular Joe. Joe is wearing a t-shirt, jeans, and tennis shoes. He's nothing special to look at, except Joe has two friends with him. Who's cooler? The well-dressed guy who appears financially successful or Joe with his two friends? Not clear yet? Well, let me expand even further.

Let's imagine Joe's two friends both have girlfriends. So, Joe is with four people now, making a group of five. You have the well-dressed guy on the left at the bar, and then you have Joe plus four friends all laughing and drinking and having a good time, making noise, attracting attention. Who is cooler now? Who will everyone want to be around? The group! This example aims to show you that if you aren't the rich guy with all the money, don't let that deter you in a social gathering because it doesn't matter.

The cool guy is the guy with all the people.

Power in Numbers

So, what if you're someone who loves being a Loner and are thinking "screw the group!" Now, there isn't anything wrong with that either, except you are reading this book to learn how to meet a woman! If that's the case, by nature, you do want a group. You are trying to meet your love and it won't work if you're off in a corner by yourself. Pay attention so you can see how you can still be you (a Loner) and find what you are looking for. This is called power in numbers.

Power and hierarchy have everything to do with your group. People may not say it, but they sense it. Everybody notices that more people equate to more power, no matter if they can help it or not.

So, what makes a person cool?

How many people validate him/her.

And what does it mean to be validated?

The cool kid wouldn't be cool unless people *agreed* he was cool. Being cool is a construct, a consideration amongst people—not an actual physical or personality trait. As an example: Do you think amongst a smart group of kids, a not-so-smart kid would be considered cool? Do you think amongst a bunch of football players, a scrawny long-distance runner would be seen as cool? No, at least not in those groups directly. The not-so-smart kid and the long-distance runner could be considered cool in other groups, but in the smart kids group and the football players group, they don't receive sufficient validation, because they are too different. The point is the subject of "cool" is merely a consideration based on others' viewpoints and where they direct their attention and admiration.

There are many times in life when what you thought was cool really wasn't, or what was once cool, isn't cool anymore. For example, slaying animals to use their skins and furs for fashion was cool in the past, definitely not cool anymore. Or now it's cool to have non-gender specific bathrooms in restaurants. Twenty years ago, that would have been very uncool. Or gas-guzzling cars where you could hear the engine roaring from down the street, guzzling one gallon for every five miles used to be cool, definitely NOT COOL now in this age of global warming. It's all about where you view something from (your viewpoint) and when (time).

So how does a person become cool? Here is your answer.

The more people **agree** that he/she is cool, the more **wanted** he/she becomes. The more wanted he/she becomes, the "**cooler**" they get. So, once again, we are talking about the **number** of people. Groups dominate, and bigger groups dominate even more. For example, a political party, once in office, will look after their agenda for the next four years. Pharmaceutical companies can push any agenda they want; they have the power and the money. If you are in school, the fraternities tend to be cool because of the sheer mass of people they have. The next time you go out into a social setting, observe the amount of attention a group generates from others, and you'll see for yourself how numbers equal power.

Before we continue, I want to talk about using money to be cool. I have seen many times, especially here in Los Angeles (and also Sri Lanka), how people have tried to use money to make them cool. That is not cool! I knew a guy who bought a Lamborghini just so people could see him in his car. He would drive up and down Sunset Boulevard (a famous street in Los Angeles) trying to pick up girls. I have actually been in the car with him as he was a good friend of my brother's and I witnessed this gimmick. I have never seen such awkward ways of attracting attention; it was so disingenuous. He was cool when he was blowing money on the girls and taking them out to fancy places, or so he thought. People took advantage of him, and he didn't know any better. He was much older than me, so I hadn't spent a lot of time with him, but I can tell you his situation did not end well for him. One night, he had a nasty run-in with some people who were tired of him showing off, and he ended up in the hospital. He attracted all the wrong people, had a girlfriend who left him after he got hospitalized, and ended up very lonely for a long period of time.

I have also seen girls who have misused men (one of them was my close friend) because they have money. The girl spent thousands of dollars at spas for massages and facials, inviting her friends to spend on her boyfriend's dime, knowing that this guy she was seeing was willing to pay for it. What happened to my friend in this situation? The girl left him the moment he put a stop to her extravagant spending. Just use this example as a lesson to know this type of "cool" will never serve you as a man to find the right girl.

Money doesn't make a man; a man makes money.

Money can be used for the pursuit of material things if that is what you want, but more importantly, money should be used to fend for your family, build a foundation for your life, and create opportunities for yourself that have long-term returns. When a woman is looking for a life partner, they are thinking about marriage and children, which means a house, school, diapers, and food. And although in this day and age, you won't have to pay for everything (unless you want to), you definitely have to put in your fair share. We are in a different era. Women aren't helpless and looking for a man to save them. In fact, it is quite the opposite; women are fierce and about their business. And with this independence, women aren't looking for you to be the sole income producer, but you at least have to put in the same as they are.

You can't fault a woman for wanting to know if you are financially secure. I have seen this as a true stress factor for men. I know a lot of men who are afraid to meet women because they aren't financially ready. Or they are embarrassed at where they are currently in life and don't want a woman to find out about it.

This has been the primary reason I have seen men fake it when they are out. Wearing special clothes, borrowing friends' cars. This is the wrong tactic. The right girl will help you build what you want to achieve in life and support you.

In my life, I have always been even more successful when I was in a steady relationship. Women ground us and make us stronger and more able. Don't think you need to have financial security or wealth before you meet your soulmate just because you believe your soulmate needs you to have it. This is false.

A huge "BUT" here—this also doesn't give you license to be broke and borrowing money from your girl either. Don't be the guy leaching off your girl, making her do everything, including paying rent and helping you get a job. Find a way you can both help each other to meet the goals you both want to achieve. This harmony of giving and receiving makes for the most fruitful relationships.

You should be well-dressed according to your standards, clean, and cordial. Well-dressed could be jeans and a t-shirt. It could be khakis and a blazer. It could be boardshorts and some sandals. I don't care what your idea of well-dressed is, but being clean, I do care about—and so will any girl. No matter your style or look, be clean. That means wipe the sleep out your eyes, comb your hair, iron your shirt, take a shower, brush your teeth. Decorum and etiquette may seem like big words only used in upper echelon circles for the uppity British, but they're not. How you conduct yourself and how you look matters in any social situation.

Etiquette is the customary code of polite behavior in society or amongst members of a particular profession or group. For

your group, whether surfers, musicians, coders, or stock/real-estate brokers, use the etiquette that applies. Decorum is behavior in keeping with good taste. Once again, when looking around at what group you are a part of, check the generally accepted ways of acting and dressing, and fall in line. A little bit of decorum and etiquette goes a LONG WAY.

And just a comment on fancy cars. Almost no one knows what type of car you drive when you go to a bar unless everyone is outside the bar (which they are not). When you are in a social setting, remember, no amount of money you have, what type of car you drive, or fancy clothes you wear is going to help you now. You are on your own with your personality and your charm. Don't be fooled by those false ideas and images you see on TV and in movies. Stay inside of your budget and buy cars that make sense for you. Now, let's get into the hierarchy and how it works.

Using Hierarchy to Your Benefit

So, how can the concept of hierarchy help you, especially if you aren't with a group or in the event you came to the bar as a Loner? First, remember the purpose of going out. People who go to a bar to socialize also have an overall goal. That goal is to meet people and be social. That is the bottom line. Remember that the **most social people** in a social gathering will be the coolest people. With that in mind, let me share an anecdote to help illustrate.

I remember when my brother and I used to go out. We had no power in numbers since it was just the two of us. However, what we had was the genuine nature of wanting to meet people just to meet people, so we went out for that reason.

Typically, we would enter together, go straight to the bar, grab a drink, and naturally walk off in different directions. I think most people call this "doing a lap" at the bar. In our first lap, we would do what I taught in Step 2, Watch and Learn. You should get into the habit of doing a lap so you can assess your surroundings. We would see each other again at the bar, hang out and chat for a minute, "catch up," then somehow naturally, we would end up doing another lap... except for this time, we were meeting people—so typically, this would take a little bit longer. Eventually, what would happen was he would meet a bunch of people at the bar, and I, having gone in the opposite direction, would meet a bunch of other people, and then he would introduce all the people he met to me, and I would do likewise.

This wasn't contrived at all. We didn't go to the bar and get a drink and walk off from each other as a plan. It just happened this way. It worked out. Now this might seem odd to you at first. But to be honest, this isn't how you might think. We didn't have a huddle, yell "break," and then go walking around the bar. It was way more organic than that. We would be ordering a drink, and I would talk to the person sitting right next to me. My brother and I would both pursue this conversation together, until at some point my bro would either realize it was too loud for him to keep sticking his ear in the conversation or naturally turn around and meet the person next to him. We didn't get up, walk around, and just meet people for the sake of meeting people as a job. Sometimes we would go to the bathroom and end up having a chat in the line. A lot of the times at bars, the girl's line is longer than the boy's line so we would talk to a girl waiting in the line while we were waiting. Or, on our way back from the bathroom, we might stop and ask a random query from someone in the bar because what they were drinking looked interesting. It was always so random and never contrived.

I don't want you to take this too literally on how to get around when you are in a social setting. You have to first affix your mind on the concept that you are there to meet people, and you will find that people will come to you! Here's something I learned from *The Secret* by Rhonda Byrne[11]. Your inner thoughts are always exposed around you. I firmly believe what exists inside of you, you will see on the outside. So, always make sure you have your intention right, and meeting people will start to flow in the most natural way you could imagine.

What was very interesting about many of these interactions was that, a lot of the time, people in groups would feel awkward about meeting a Loner guy because they didn't want him to be the hanger-on of the group. But this would quickly get nullified because when we introduced the people we previously met to each other, they perceived we weren't looking to invade their group. But still, we are only two in number, so *how did we create power in numbers and really enable the hierarchy to work for us?*

We started introducing the random people we met to one another.

Introducing people to others is a great way to start building your hierarchy. I have noticed in most social settings that there is a little bit of an awkward feeling that people get when introducing people to other people. I've been in situations with friends where they just forget to do it all together. I have also witnessed within the last year of being at over 100 venues to sing (mostly bars), that when you show up at a bar solo, you start meeting

11 Byrne, Rhonda. *The Secret*. New York: Atria Books, 2018.

people, and even the people who came with a friend don't introduce the person they are standing right next to them. So, what
I have done to create some camaraderie is introduce a random
artist I met to another random artist I met, and then they finally
introduce their friend. People aren't doing this maliciously, but
you have to imagine that not everyone knows social cues or is
interested in talking to others. Also, with the myriad of back-
grounds you will run into in life, there is no telling why this
doesn't happen, but it also doesn't matter. You live your life in
the way you know best.

You do, however, want to be wary of who you are introducing
to each other. There could be times when you meet people and
they just aren't nice, but you only find this out on your second
or third round of "touch and go" at the bar or wherever you are.
Those people should not be propagated around at a function.
Toxic people infuse a whole crowd with their negative energy.
Let's take a bottle of clean water. One small piece of mud inside
the water and it is no longer drinkable. This is the same with
toxic people; they are like weeds in your yard or like a splinter
in your finger. Damn splinter is so small, but it hurts so much!
Don't ever be reasonable with toxic people. They should be naturally weeded out if you are using the step of "touch and go"
because you would have the opportunity to find this out after a
second or third go-round

Continuing my story from earlier, as all this is going on in
the bar with my brother and I, usually our cousin and some girlfriends would have met us at the bar by then, and all of our
friends would eventually meet these new people we met. Five
times out of 10, we would actually end up sharing a table or

intermingling with these groups and have a grand old time with many new friends.

Remember that you create your power by what you say and do. However, having a group creates strength! People like to feel accepted, and group events achieve that because of camaraderie and group understanding. This is the reason most of the pastimes we see in the world are group events. It is a great feeling to be around other people. Find a great group of friends that support you and make you a better person, and it will pay off tenfold within a social setting.

For those who don't have a lot of good friends and/or love to go out alone, you can build a group right at the event you're at. Building groups instantaneously at the event gives you the advantage of harnessing the power of the hierarchy.

You, the Lone Ranger at the bar, meet a couple of Stragglers. Well, at the right time, introduce one Straggler to the other, and since you were the connection, they would suspect this is your group (both sides), which basically serves the same purpose. I've done this so many times but not realizing this very fact—that the people I introduced to each other actually think I am a part of each other's group. I tend to only find that out later. Of course, exercise caution, as you don't want to lie or be inauthentic. Usually, people would ask me later on in the night how I knew "so and so" and I would say that we just met… but honestly, by then everyone is drunk and having a good time so we jokingly would make up some truly concocted lie like, "We met scuba diving in Egypt." The look on their faces was always pretty classic. If I had a dollar for every time… ah, forget it.

People don't mind being introduced to new people, but everything should be out and open on the table. That is **not** to say that you have to say in the beginning of an introduction between one random to another random: "I just met the both of you." But when asked, never lie. I have randomly introduced Randoms to each other so many times wherein I received nothing out of it, because once again I had nothing I truly was looking to gain but some good conversation.

But know that having a group and knowing how to leverage it is a strength to be reckoned with. And with this new information about how to create power in numbers, you can rise in the hierarchy, effectively turning that typically outward flow, inward back to you!

Step 5

DIVERSIFY YOUR RISK

S o, what does it mean to diversify your risk? In investing, it means don't put all your money into one investment. Simply, don't risk everything on the success of one venture! Money has value and, like money, so do you. In fact, you are the most valuable thing you have! Your time, affection, interest, and communication with another person is *very* valuable, so don't waste it when at a function or gathering with just one person. Give yourself the chance to meet lots of people.

I remember multiple occasions where me and the boys would hang, and I'd see them scan the room, find a girl they like, and proclaim, "That's the one, that's the one right there!"

Then all night they try to figure out how to meet this ONE girl! Most of the time, the outcome is grim—either they never meet this girl, or they meet the girl and she just isn't interested. I've watched as friends of mine have ultimately gotten so let down and, frankly, it is sad. Let's talk about how to fix this problem of getting bogged down or fixated on one girl at a function.

How do you get let down? Are there mechanics involved, or is this just a part of life? When you try and meet a girl at a function and it doesn't go right, what actually happened?

Expectation!

You wanted it so bad, built up an expectation to get it, and then got let down when it didn't happen as you thought. First, don't paint a picture of your ideal woman in your head when you are out at a social gathering. Second, go back Step 1 and see if you really got your approach right. If you scan the room for only women, you do not have it right.

Think about the qualities you are looking for: same interests, same love/hate for things and types of people. Don't be deceived by the outer shell and then think you have to squish all those qualities you are looking for into the "hot" girl of the night. Of course, you **must** be attracted to the person you want to spend the rest of your life with because for us men we are very visual, but looks will never be your highest priority when you are looking for a life partner (explained thoroughly in Step 7).

Women are more level-headed when it comes to looks versus qualities as they (for the most part) look for the *right* guy, not just the hot guy. If he is hot, that is definitely a plus, but intuitively I would say women definitely search out qualities much more than we as men do. Nevertheless, don't come to a social gathering with an expectation, come to a social gathering to mix and be social with no expectations.

Expectations get you caught up in thinking something should be a certain way. You already painted some picture in your mind of how this is supposed to go down, and you're mentally pushing to see it go down exactly that way. That doesn't work! Rhonda Byrne, the author of *The Secret*, tells us to say what you want and let the Universe figure out **how** it is going to give it to you. I agree. There is some level chance you have to allow for. But that also doesn't mean you just sit around and wait for the girl of your dreams to come to you. You have to take action, but it doesn't have to be as direct as you may think. You will meet her but be patient. Go through your steps as I have written them, and you will meet her. It may not be **how** you imagined, but it will happen. I don't want to be too hokey and/or spiritual at this moment, so I am going to give you some science to back up my statement.

The second law of thermodynamics, which is also called the law of entropy, proves that being proactive (e.g. going out and meeting people) can enable the "powers" of the universe to bring you what you want in an indirect way. Entropy is defined as "the number of ways a system can be arranged." More entropy means not only more ways a system can be arranged, but more ways a system can become disordered.[12]

Let's say you have a bag of marbles. Well, if you take a marble out and put it on the table, there is only one way it can

---

12   Cardenas, Richard. "What Is Entropy? - Definition, Law & Formula." STUDY.
COM. Accessed April 28, 2020. https://study.com/academy/lesson/what-is-
entropy-definition-law-formula.html.

be arranged. When you take the next one out, there are two ways it could be arranged. The more marbles you take out of the bag, the more ways in which these marbles can be arranged. So, with three, maybe four, marbles you can handle the different arrangements you can put the marbles in. You can say there is **still** a good level of order. But if you put ten marbles (each marble you add creates more entropy) on the table, this order can become very disorderly as there are a multitude of different combinations, and it gets overwhelming.[13]

In most scientific systems, you don't want entropy because you want to be able to have order so you always know what's happening and can have control over a hypothesis or project. In a social setting, you want disorder (this should not be seen as disorderly or something negative) because you want to create the ability to have a multitude of different possible outcomes for which even you could not predict. You want the conversation you are having with a male Straggler to lead you to a conversation you eventually have with the hot girl who is currently outside with her friends waiting to come into the bar.

Imagine that every time you meet someone at a function, you are creating a "touch point," adding another "marble" (adding entropy) onto the table of this social gathering. The more "touch points" you add, the more entropy you add to the system (this function), leaving its outcome more and more random and up to chance. My point is that the more people you meet at a function or party makes your random interactions go up. This, in turn, makes who you might meet for the night way less predictable. This is all to say that having expectations when so many vari-

---

13   Ibid.

ables can elicit who knows what kind of result is not only silly, but a surefire way to be disappointed.

Managing Expectations

Let's talk about this point of expectation and wanting something to happen in a certain way. Have you ever been caught up on a girl before or got caught up with a life goal? I know I have! My definition of "caught up" here means either stuck on or slowed down. Getting stuck is sticky. This goal you are trying to achieve has you caught up, in essence, "sticking" you. In social gatherings, when you are out and about at a party or function, you don't want to get sticky—meaning stuck to expectations and how things "should" go.

How do we accomplish not getting sticky? Let's say you arrive at a social function or bar, and you see a girl who is unbelievable. Before you dive so deep into fantasizing about her and the children you're going to have, find your way to the bar, grab a drink, and talk to someone else immediately. Or if you aren't at a bar, find your way outside the function, even if it's the bathroom, take a couple of deep breaths, get some perspective, and then come back in and give the party a brand-new scan. Take a fresh look at the party and the people in it, like you haven't seen it before in a new unit of time.

You need to stay in the present moment, but keep moving forward! I have walked into a bar before and gotten mesmerized by a girl. She keeps looking at me or I keep looking at her. It is completely distracting. So, I check myself and see if I'm living my true intention. Sometimes, I will just walk up and say hi to this girl, because I can feel she is calling me. But if it's only you doing the staring and she doesn't notice you at all, that is stalker status. This is when you need to take that bathroom break and give yourself a moment.

Just like performing "touch and go" with the individual people you meet, in this instance you are performing "touch and go" on the overall function. You arrive at the function ("touch"), but then you go outside ("go") and leave the function for a moment to get a breather. Then you return to the function ("touch" again). This tactic of "touch and go" on the actual function can be very helpful because it gives you some time and space to gain perspective.

When a person gets "caught up," their energetic flow gets slowed down or stopped, and the only way this can happen is with some level of mass. About 2,500 years ago, the Buddha taught that all thought is connected to mass (mental mass that is). For example, when you feel depressed, you feel like the world is on your shoulders; you feel heavy. Conversely, when you are happy you feel light, like you can jump and touch the sky! In these examples above, where you got caught up, this is you with a ton of mass. In fact, if you were to break down mass even further, you would find that all mass vibrates. If it vibrates, then it has a frequency.

The Germans have long proved this concept with the invention of vibrational therapy to heal the body[14]. They discovered decades ago that there's a spectrum of frequencies at which every single bone, muscle, and organ vibrates. Amazingly, they have created incredible healing machines that operate on and target frequencies,

---

14   "History and Scientific Origins." Vibrate Fitness, March 10, 2018. https://www. vibratefitness.com/scientific-origins-of-vibration-fitness/.

which are being used to this day. These machines measure physical mass. However, when you get stuck on a girl or something else you want or when you feel depressed, this is mental mass.

This mental mass is what "catches up" people. This mass could be in the form of memory. When you are remembering something for that moment, you are no longer in present time. You have stopped being present to look back at something in the past. Memories are the makeup of our relationship to life and are very important, but definitely not important in a social gathering. You have to stay in the present time in order to be the best you and to make sure you aren't living out something from the past while you are in the present.

For example, say you see a girl at a party and her long, flowing hair reminds you of Megan Fox in the first *Transformers* where she pops the hood to explain to Shia LaBeouf how his engine works. Or her beautiful complexion reminds you of Halle Berry's glistening skin when she was coming out of the ocean in *Die Another Day*. Catch yourself because you are not in the present time. Plus, you're concocting expectations based on a fabricated movie.

I have gone to bars multiple times where friends of mine would say, "I don't want to go there" and I would ask why, and they would tell me about a breakup they had there or some memory that makes them sad. That place isn't sad. Your past connection to it is! Don't mix up your memories of the past with things and people in the present. If you are there in the present, then you can look at every place (even old places) like new places and every experience like new experiences. I wake up and see my girlfriend every day. I don't ever imagine when I see her in the morning, "oh, I know what this is." When I see my girl every morning, I think today is a new day (I also think "damn, she's beautiful") and this is going to be a new experience with her, and we can create it any which way we like.

It makes life a lot more fun when you don't allow yourself to get bogged down by the situations of yesterday and stay in the present. You have the right to create anything in your life and future. You possess this power. If something is getting you down, create right over it!

"Creating Over"

What does it mean to create over something? Let's say someone is telling you that you can't get a certain job. How do you create over that? You send out letters to that company asking for an interview. You do your research on the CEO there and find a way to get in contact with that person. You check LinkedIn; you find resourceful ways to meet people who may know people in that company. You can even walk right into their Human Resources and tell them you are serious about getting that job. You look at the prerequisites of getting that job and make sure you have done them all. You can and WILL get that job.

Anything can be accomplished at any age for any reason. I can be the first one to tell you that from experience. I spent most of my musical career as a rapper. I then decided to switch over to singing. I was already in my thirties, and my friends told me I was a fool. They all knew I couldn't hold a freaking note! I was not trained in music and had never gone to school for it. So how did I learn? I sang! I studied voice, I took classes, I enrolled in the Musicians Institute's Vocal Program, I sang, I joined a church choir, I sang, and then I sang some more! One year of school, over 100 live gigs later, not to mention countless live streams and online videos, I can sing. There is nothing a person cannot do.

Here's another example of creating over something. Let's say you get into a breakup and you feel you could never meet another girl like her. Well, how do you create over this? Well, you go out and follow these steps and meet a ton of people. You diversify your risk and join groups and networks and start putting yourself out there. We still have Steps 6 and 7 to get through, so I won't cover those here, but you do all the steps laid out as I have written them. With these steps done, you will end up with a ton of new friends, and somewhere in the middle of all this creation, you will find an even better girl.

You can create your circumstances and your life by being productive and creating in whatever space you want to see results in. If you are a painter, paint. If you are a writer, write. If you are a coder, code! Application and persistence of what you want is how you achieve it. When you are at an outing, you are creating your situation at that moment, in essence, creating an environment inside of this environment. Remember this power to create is in your hands because at the end of the day, you have the bare-bones ability to simply talk to another person.

This may seem like it takes effort at first, but this is only because you are stuck to yesterday's ways of operating within a social gathering. We can relate this to water. One of the best quotes I have read comes from one of my favorite people, Bruce Lee:

"Empty your mind, be formless. Shapeless—like water.
If you put water into a cup, it becomes the cup. You put

*water into a bottle and it becomes the bottle. You put it
in a teapot, it becomes the teapot."*
—Bruce Lee

When water takes form, it doesn't take effort. Effort takes force, and force will never get you anywhere in a social setting because people don't like awkward run-ins that don't feel natural.

What happens when you get stuck on someone or hang around too long in your first interaction? You are forcing something. Let's say a friend introduced me to a bunch of girls at a table, and I introduce myself, and then all of a sudden, it gets quiet. I start to get the feeling they don't really want me there as I am the one dude who isn't sitting down at the table, and they are all eating. You can see what an awkward position I'm in, can't you? So, it is time to bounce!

I remember when I was a kid and I would be rough with my Legos, or screwed something in too hard, or slammed a door, my dad would always tell me not to use force because he knew it was futile. Of course, I didn't listen. Why would I listen to him? Referring back to Step 3, his advice was free, so it no longer had value to me. #realtalk

What is the outcome of playing rough with Legos? The Legos fly out of your hands. What is the outcome of screwing something in with too much force? You strip the screw. How about closing a door by using too much force? It slams—or there just might be something in the way that you just smashed.

This remains true in a social gathering as well; too much force only makes things awkward. You think force will give you the result you want, and faster, but in reality, you push circumstances (or objects) too fast, and they grind. This creates stress, which results in a botched first interaction, a lost opportunity, or even worse—someone thinking less of you than who you really are.

Let's take a closer look at using force versus not using force.

Using Force

You see a girl you want to talk to. You wait around the bar and don't really talk to too many people as you are waiting for your moment to pounce. It's a little later in the night by now because you have been waiting for the right moment and BOOM! The moment has opened up and you b-line it straight to her. What happens? You say hi and introduce yourself. You guys are chatting, it's all working out, then... another BOOM! Some guy from one of the groups that you DIDN'T connect with, let's call him Eric, notices your dream girl and runs over and says hi to his old friend. She greets him profusely. What does he do then? He drags her over to "his" friends, and you get left behind! Final BOOM! Sorry, man. This is how it works.

Not Using Force

Let's look at the same situation, but this time, using my steps.

First, you re-check your approach (Step 1), realize you came to meet people, NOT just women. You find a cool dude who seems to be on the same page as you (Step 2). You walk over and say, "Hi," make your introduction and leave (Step 3). You repeat Step 3 at least three times. Then, after you've done a couple rounds on Step 3, you introduce some Stragglers to each other (Step 4).

Now you are sitting around chatting with a bunch of new people you just connected with, and all of a sudden, Eric, one of the guys in your new group, says, "Oh shoot, is that Suzie over there? Snap!" He runs over to her and says, "Hi!!" He brings her back to his friends and introduces her to everyone, which

includes you, because you are now a new friend. She hangs around to meet and chat with all of Eric's friends.

WAIT, is that the girl you were trying to meet when you just walked in?? YES! This is Step 5, my friend, working its magic. This is Step 5 being carried through without force!

Diversifying your risk is about meeting more people, and meeting more people creates randomity, per the law of entropy, which I explained above. I'm sure you have heard the story of an artist playing at some random place and getting discovered, or the story of someone making a video on YouTube and it blows up with millions of views overnight. These miracles definitely do happen, but most of the time, it isn't exactly like that. YouTube stars typically make hundreds of videos before the one that catches on and garners millions of views. Artists getting discovered in the bar probably played hundreds of shows in many, many bars and clubs—most of the time, unpaid.

What they did was keep moving and creating opportunities to get discovered, and one day they do get discovered. Ed Sheeran played more than 250 shows in one year before he got "discovered." Katy Perry was an artist for 10 years under a completely different name before she was discovered. Taylor Swift was a country artist first, before she became a Pop Phenom. Justin Timberlake and Ariana Grande were both Disney kids, so they've been in entertainment for decades. These people put in time and work! So have faith in the process. You need to put yourself out there to get something back in return, because the more you communicate your message, the more it gets heard. What you focus on grows. Dwayne "The Rock" Johnson said it best:

> *"When you focus on you, you grow.*
> *When you focus on shit, shit grows."*
> —Dwayne Johnson

What you do over and over again you inevitably get better at. Imagine you couldn't dribble a basketball. Spend 30 minutes a night dribbling, and I am sure you will get better. When you are meeting all these people using Step 3 (Touch and Go) and Step 5 (Diversify Your Risk), you are practicing and focusing on what you want. So, your ability to meet people and the breadth of your connections will grow.

You are repeating the art of having non-threatening conversations and being yourself while doing it. You are pulling into you, your original intention, which is to meet the girl of your dream! So, with all these "touch points" you create by diversifying your risk and your intention in place, you better believe things will come your way.

> *"One day you will wake up and there won't be*
> *any more time to do the things you've always*
> *wanted to do. Do it now!"*
> —Paulo Coelho. Author, *The Alchemist*

There is no real secret here—**just an act of consistent courage to be you every time you are out with people**.

So remember, you want to meet LOTS of people, not just pinpoint the one or two you want to meet and, thus, bank all your success on those two people. That strategy will leave you disappointed. You want to spread yourself out so to speak, meet lots of people, and make it known across many people who you are.

The more you diversify your risk, the more people you meet. The more people you meet, the more people who know you. The more people who know you, the easier it becomes to meet new people. And eventually, amongst all those new people you are meeting, you are bound to meet a great girl. It's all but guaranteed to happen!

Remember, the environment plays a huge role in interactions, so don't ever discount yourself because on a particular night you didn't get what you were expecting. But like I mentioned at the beginning of this step, don't walk into a social gathering with expectations. Just be fluid like water and go with the flow.

So, diversify your risk! Meet other people. Meet other girls. Meet other guys. Go out to go out. Don't go out just to meet girls. You never know where the right one actually is, and you never know how or what is going to happen. The world will take you everywhere… Don't resist—go!

I learned this lesson the hard way so many times when I was stuck on things I wanted career-wise. I wanted to be a famous rapper in America so badly. I spent tons of money on promotions for a song that hit #1 on MTV's Most Popular Music Videos chart above Lil Wayne and Taylor Swift. But I forced it and found all the wrong people, who then stole money from me and sent my rap career in America crashing to the floor!

Luckily for me, I have never been this way with people and, to this day, I have never had a problem meeting anyone.

To diversify, walk around the social gathering you are at and try to meet at least five new people when you go out, guys or girls. Remember, no person lives on an island by themselves. Everyone has friends. Go out, diversify, meet more than just the one you feel you really wanted to hit it off with. Also note— most of the time when a woman sees a man speaking to multiple people, they get the feeling this person (you, that is) is popular. Remember how we previously defined "cool" in Step 4 in a social setting? Being seen talking to multiple people in and of itself will make women (or anybody) want to talk to you more because we're social creatures, specifically in our celebrity and social media-crazed age.

Being open gives you the highest chance of getting what you want. Trust me—for finding the right girl, this works. If it doesn't work, you have already diversified, so it won't feel as bad if that random girl at the bar doesn't want to talk to you.

> *"Anything you can imagine you can create."*
> —Oprah Winfrey

Imagine your life and create how you want it.

Step 6
BUILD YOUR NETWORK

B uild a network?? Shit, that's hard! It's forced and not fun. Going to a place where everyone has a freaking name tag and trying to introduce yourself? Hell, no! *I am not a salesman. I don't have the time.*

Yes, when talking about building a network, I have heard these excuses, but I am not talking about building a network for work. I am not talking about putting on name tags with your full name, company position, and logo splattered all over it, and the awkward handshakes that go along with it. I am talking about building a network for play! To do fun things, like go out, mountain bike, surf, read, bar hop. Stuff like that!

And then you say, well I don't have time for fun, I have work, the gym, then I need to eat, walk my dog, and by that time the night is over. Oh yes, I have also heard this before. To this I say, tough news buddy if you don't have time for fun you definitely don't have time for a girlfriend! So, make time!

How Do You Make Time?

Let me tell you.

When I started off in the workforce after college, I worked in my family business. I was never meant for real estate, though this is where I ended up after school. In high school, I was a DJ, in college a music producer, and when I started working for my dad, I was making my first album as a rapper. Now, working in the family business is never a 9-5, because you have the responsibility of ownership, and you're always expected to put in more time for the sake of the family. So, when there is a homeless guy shitting in your emergency stairwell, **you** have to kick him out. When you need more supplies to do a job, **you** go get it. When some tenant is smoking weed in the building, **you** have to go talk to them, when the fire alarm goes off in the building for no reason at 1:00 am, **you** have to show up. In hindsight, if I wanted more time, I would have been better off working a non-family 9-5.

On top of this, we were $700,000 deep in Accounts Payable. Yes, we owed other vendors who did work for us almost $1 million dollars, and every month we were losing $40,000! We were completely insolvent. I didn't create these problems; this situation was given to me when I took the job. I should have been completely stressed out! Could you imagine that I would even have any time to do anything else? No! But I did.

During this same time, I wrote, recorded, and released my first album, and by the end of the year, I had a #1 hip hop hit in Sri Lanka, my country of origin. So, how did I do it? How did I make time to do two completely different trades at the same time and excel in both? Here's how...

I was up at 7:00 am (I lived close to work, a downtrodden apartment in MacArthur Park in Los Angeles). I worked from 8:00 am to 8:00 pm, barring any random events that happened, like fire alarms going off or break-ins. Then, I'd jump over to the gym for a workout. After that, I went straight to the studio and started recording my album. I would usually be there until 1:00 am or 2:00 am. I did this *every day*. I didn't think about whether I could do it or how I could do it. I just did it.

So, what happened? Well, in four months, I cut the deficit in the building to $0. We no longer were losing that $40,000 every month. I also finished and released my first album.

What happened in one year? I cut the payables down. You remember that $700,000? I cut that down to zero. This means I paid off ALL the vendors who hadn't gotten paid for years. In my music, after that one-year mark, I had a #1 hit in Sri Lanka, a song that became a classic on the island, called "Jeevithye," which was added to YES FM's relief CD, *Heal Sri Lanka*[15], for the tsunami that ravaged the country.

But it didn't stop there. I continued stacking the odds in my favor by doing this for 7 years straight. What happened in 7 years? I raised the value of the real estate by 150%, putting over $5 million cash in my dad's hands. I won Best Rap Performance

---

15   DeLon. *Heal Sri Lanka*. Maharaja Entertainments PVT LTD, 2014, compact disc. https://music.apple.com/us/album/jeevithye/806163668?i=806163709.

in our MTV awards (we don't have a Grammy award show, so this was like winning best rapper in the country). I put out three albums, two mixtapes, and got a #1 right here in the U.S. on MTV's Most Popular Music Videos.

You don't make time by trying to figure out where to put things. You make time by NOT wasting it! I don't spend time on my phone looking at Instagram. I don't wake up, then hang out in my bed for 30 minutes. I try not to travel during traffic hours. I don't watch TV. I don't ponder how something won't work. I don't second guess my dreams. I don't eat foods that make me tired. I cut out the bullshit.

Maintaining Focus

Okay, those are the things I didn't do. Now, let me tell you what I *did* do.

I did things that kept me focused and the #1 thing that kept me focused was eating right and going to the gym. These two things go hand in hand. Working out is so incredibly important! Your body is your engine, and if you don't put the right gas into the engine and use it, it will ultimately stall and break down. What does it mean to put the right gas into the engine? Eat right. Eat healthy. Don't eat fast food, don't eat fries, don't drink soda, don't eat cake. Put the right gas into the engine and it burns like butane fuel. You should be exploding with energy from the food you eat. Eating bad food is equivalent to putting water into your engine instead of gas. Doesn't eating fried rice and a bunch of sweet and sour chicken from a Chinese restaurant make you want to take a nap? YES! What if you ate some fresh salmon with salad? How would you feel then? GREAT! After this, let's say you went out and ran a mile instead of sitting at home watching porn?

Working out and eating healthy are the first steps to making sure you are in the present and alert so you are able to do the things you want to do in life. Your body is tied to your efficiency and your alertness. You want to accomplish as much as you can with your time, so you must keep a strong mental state. Being in this strong mental state will help you keep your integrity while achieving your goals.

You don't need to make it your life, but working out is very underrated. Just that one-hour workout I got in almost every day of my life since college has kept me alive, energetic, and young. To this day, I get compliments on how young I look and how energetic I am. I am constantly being asked my secret. Well, you are reading it! Working out is almost as important as sleep to me.

Building a Network

Now let's talk about building a network. Networks depend on people to stay thriving. A network isn't a network without its individual members, and not only that, but the network needs to coordinate together in order to sustain and grow; it's a cooperative effort with interested members co-creating it.

Let's use Wi-Fi networks as an example here. When you want the internet, your internet company comes to your place to set it up, right? Yes. They bring a modem that is used to access the internet line from the street. They also bring a router, which is connected to the modem and is used to distribute the internet to house members, usually using Wi-Fi.

Just as you need the modem to get access to the internet line, to get access to people, you will need a "people line." How do you get this people line? By finding activities of your liking to expose you to more people. Your line into more people are activities like a cooking class, soccer team, or book club.

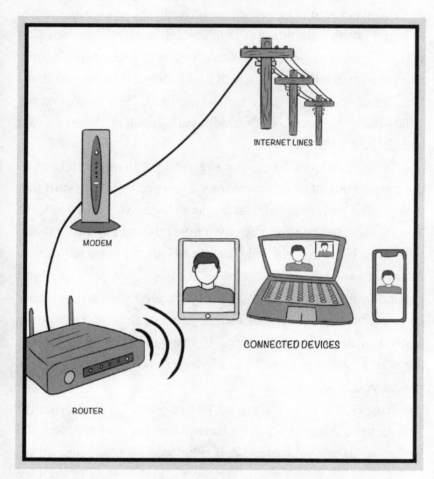

Well, how do you choose these activities? Ask yourself what do you like to do? Or what would you like to try?

Don't ask yourself *where the women are*. Or *what hot girls like to do*.

This approach, once again, equals fail!

You want to meet people you have things in common with. If you look for activities *you like*, such as reading, then you will find people on this "line" that you will **genuinely** become friends with. Remember to always be genuine. Maybe you don't like lots of things, so... try something new! How do you know what you like if you haven't tried it yet? Reach out into this vast world and try things!

As children, we literally put everything into our mouths until our parents taught us otherwise or we learned by eating stuff that was gross. Our level of curiosity was so high, we wanted to learn everything. By fostering your own interests and exploring them, you bring back this childlike nature of curiosity, which in turn naturally broadens your circles of friends. On top of this, you expand your knowledge on the subject. Doing an activity and/ or learning about a subject brings you to action and causation instead of no action and effect. If you want something in life, the way to get it is to be "cause" over it, not effect, and action makes you cause.

Why is it that as time goes on we wane in our curiosity? People have become so complacent with life and uninterested in the world around them. Their relationships suck, they resort to beer and TV every night. What we see around us is what we shouldn't do. Have you ever watched the news and said to yourself, "I feel so much happier now"? NO! Because fear is the method of choice in mainstream media. All of the news channels only give bad news, instilling fear in our everyday lives and surroundings. If it is not the war going on the Middle East, which by the way has been going since I was born, then it is about the unjust Communism in China or nuclear weapons testing in North Korea, or the death toll from gang members in your area or that sex abuser down the street or... you get the picture. This is the stock in trade of the NEWS! News is meant to suppress and scare you. Suppress you from feeling great, scare you into never leaving your house, locking your doors, not trusting your fellow man. The news puts you in a state of fear, and man in a state of fear is easy to control!

On top of this, a couple of bad relationships are enough to make you not want to traverse old bars. A couple of injuries make you not want to work out anymore. A couple of bad jobs make you not want to reach for your dreams. Pretty soon you resort to beer and TV. But don't let your curiosity wane on account of the garbage around you and your past misfortunes. Don't let "the man" beat you!

You need to put all that aside, as discovery is how we advance as a society. If Thomas Edison didn't keep reaching for his vision, we wouldn't have the light bulb. If Henry Ford didn't push his team to put six cylinders in one engine block, we wouldn't have the modern engine. It's been said by Rhonda Byrne, author of *The Secret*, Napoleon Hill, author of *Think and Grow Rich,* and the billionaire himself, Andrew Carnegie, that *your thoughts become things*.

Put your attention on good things. Believe you can do it. Be a part of the great people of this world who have discovered and invented all we use today, from the light bulb to the internet. Networking = discovery. The discovery of new people, places, and ideas. Networking is part and parcel of the fabric of man, because it is through this we find new ideas, meet new people, and grow! Don't be afraid to try new things and find new ways and methods of living your life. This is the genuine nature of which I have been speaking about since Step 1.

Be True to Yourself

Here is what I don't want you to do…

I don't want you to choose something like yoga as an interest only because you know it usually has many more women than men. What happens when you make this blunder?

You meet a girl on false pretenses; she believes you are something you are not and eventually she finds you out and realizes you two aren't on the same page. But let's say you dated for one year and now you are breaking up. This is one year of your life wasted for some disingenuous move you made at a yoga studio. This does happen. Trust me, I have been witness to it.

Plus, do you really want to keep up an untruth with your partner? Your potential future wife? Your relationship thrives when you have things in common. What you both genuinely love stands the test of time. Don't waste time on false pretense as you will pay for this later. It ends in a broken relationship or an unhappy one.

What is the first practical step to doing this?

Find the things you love and do those things.

How do you do this?

Pull up the internet, get on Google and find groups that do those things you like. There are Facebook groups, Instagram hashtags, and websites like Meetup.com or LinkedIn. But the most simple way to do it is a straight-up Google search! "Book club near me." "Cooking classes near me." I do this all the time. In fact, I just joined a new CrossFit gym in the area I now live in just so I can get acquainted with some new people. I love to work out, so it fits into my realm of activities that I genuinely love, and I love being part of a team sport. So, it was very natural for me, and after being in class only one day, I was already invited to go watch some CrossFit games with some people from my class.

I also began doing a ton of open mics in the area to get acquainted with the artists in the area. Being a musician is also in the realm of things I genuinely love. Once again, very natural to me.

In terms of branching out and doing things that aren't in my wheelhouse, I have joined a multitude of volunteer communities and offered my services as a teacher for kids all the way up to high school students. I have met some fantastic new people in this area, and it has given me some really great ideas on how to help better the educational system here in the United States. Not to mention it has expanded my network of friends and women quite a bit. There are a multitude of different ways you can find networks and a multitude of networks. So, do a little research (but don't overthink it) and dive in.

Another very important point about networks, in the absence of having a significant other, is that these are the groups you turn to for fun times, serious times, and, above all, to create great long-lasting relationships. In the past, I had networks for every type of thing I liked. When I was young, I was very curious about learning about other cultures because I found language and customs from different nations quite fascinating. In college, I was part of the Black Student Association, the Chinese American Student Association, the Latin Business Association, and a couple more—and I am none of those races. What I found out when I joined these groups is that they all accepted me as their friend. I was literally their "token" in every situation. But, they had a lot of respect for me because they knew I genuinely wanted to learn more about their cultures.

It did so happen that, at a Latin Business Student Association dinner, I sat across from one of the most beautiful girls I had ever seen at the time. We sat and talked that night, becoming fast friends. We found out in that conversation that we were in some of the same classes and, after that night, we made a friend date to meet up after class and shoot the shit. This happened for months, and we became really close friends. One thing led to another and we fell in love (of which I'll explain in Step 7 on how to move a

friendship into a love relationship). She was my college sweetheart! This is how it happens, boys!

When I got out of college, I naturally ended up with quite a few different groups of friends/networks. I had my going out buddies, music buddies, DJ friends, real estate buddies, Sri Lankan buddies, and workout buddies. It's quite interesting when you have lots of groups of friends, all from different walks of life.

You end up becoming the "router" for the "people lines" you created. Your line into multiple modems or "people lines" makes **you** the router! Because now people will come to you to meet other people. I will diagram this out so it is properly illustrated.

See, most people stick to their groups and their friends, and they don't usually branch out. Well, if you are the one who does it, then they begin to depend on you to open their world! It is a gift to be able to know people from all different walks of life, as it expands your knowledge, your wisdom, your tolerance, and your happiness.

This is the meaning of building a network. People are amazing, and there is not a single person on this earth, from the beggar on the streets of Colombo (the capital of Sri Lanka) to the richest man flying on a private jet who you couldn't learn something from. Truly. Learning from books can give you knowledge just as learning from others' experiences can… but the latter is way more fun!

Build a Network. Imagine it as building a team of people who are vying for your success in life. All the people you meet who share the same interests as you also want the same things you do: a fruitful life with great friends and family. The more you get out there and build a network, the more people you will meet, and the more people you meet, the more women you will meet. And the more women you meet, the more comfortable you will become around women. And the more comfortable you are around women, the easier your interactions will be with women, and the easier your interactions are, the more **you**, you become. So, in that moment when you are the most comfortable you, and you meet a girl who likes you, you will know you have the right girl because she loves you for the real you!

Step 7

KNOW WHAT YOU ARE LOOKING FOR AND HAVE FUN!

T hus far, we have covered what **you** need to do to meet girls. How your intention is KEY when you approach. How "watch and learn" makes your interaction genuine and smooth. How to not overstay your welcome by "touch and go." We've also gone over how groups affect how you are viewed in a social gathering and how to use it to your advantage. We covered expectations, not putting all your eggs in one basket and, lastly, creating more opportunities to meet women by building networks. Well, at this point, you know *how* to meet her!

If you have used the method thus far, by now you probably have created a friendship with her and, hopefully, even gone out a couple times with her. Now, in this last step, I want to talk about what **she** should have to make her valuable to YOU!

What I notice most with men when it comes to meeting women is that we see a woman's outer shell *far* before we see anything else. In fact, in a study conducted by economist Raymond Fisman and colleagues for Columbia University[16], 392 single men and women were invited to participate in a speed-dating event. Participants went on speed dates with members of the opposite sex. In this study, attractiveness mattered far more to potential mates than intelligence. A one-point increase in a woman's attractiveness rating (on a 1 to 10 scale) boosted the chances that a man would want to see her again by an average of 14 percentage points.

How a woman looks becomes the most important part. We connect having a hot girl to our own self-esteem. They give us bragging rights and, for some of us, the hotter the girl, the more self-worth we feel!

No, no, no. Malarkey!

Her looks are important for sure, but it's DEFINITELY NOT the most important. Yes, principally, you must have physical attraction because without it you won't continue to pursue a relationship. But hinging a relationship on looks alone leaves wide open gaps in the relationship because you don't spend a relationship looking at someone. You live life with someone, and

---

16   Milkman, Katherine L. "In Experiments, Researchers Figured out What Men and Women Really Want in a Mate." *The Washington Post*, February 12, 2018. https://www.washingtonpost.com/news/wonk/wp/2018/02/12/in-experiments-researchers-figured-out-what-men-and-women-really-want-in-a-mate/.

that includes activities, goals, problems, wins, losses, friends, family, kids, etc.

Don't fall into the trap of seeing a hot girl and then trying to make her fit all the requirements you have for a woman. The classic square peg in a round hole situation. I have fallen into the trap of pursuing and dating girls before because I thought they were hot, only to recant with some serious regrets as she was not what I wanted, which broke my heart and wasted my time! These were relationships I "fell" into. I met her out, she was hot, I wanted more and so did she. It was easy and convenient, I saw some signs, I ignored them. Ultimately, we became an item, it was easy and convenient, and then time passed and shit got real, we stumbled around, and we got disappointed.

There is a little bit of strategy here. Let me ask you this. Would you start a business with someone based on how pretty they are? No. I hope not anyway! Then why do you start the most important relationship in your life based upon looks? It's illogical.

I can understand in this era how hard it is to see the other traits of a potential partner with the advent of dating apps, when the first thing you see is how a woman looks. Dating apps focus primarily on looks. This prevents you from seeing what you are really looking for.

Dump the Apps

I have used a couple of apps before and I realized that I, too, was falling into the trap of just looking at girls' outer shells, and this was giving me a disingenuous feeling. I found myself spending HOURS on an app, sitting on my couch, scrolling through girls as if I was shopping for household goods on Amazon.

Pretty girl—swipe right. Less attractive girl—swipe left. Pretty girl—right. Slovenly girl—left. Left, Right. Right, Left. Right. Felt like a rote military drill: I was going through motions that kept me mindlessly busy, but I was getting nowhere. And after I'd swipe my thumb into oblivion, I'd get a response here, a response there. Then I pursued awkward conversations, because the women don't want to meet a psycho so you have to be extra friendly and contrived in your text messaging. On top of the fact that text messages don't convey any sort of emotions so you can't interpret the emotion of the communication as well as you would if you heard them in person, which again can leave you in a mystery. Then the "meet up," for a drink, because lunch or dinner might take too long if you don't like them. Ultimately, it felt so rehearsed. I felt like I was being interviewed. These interactions just didn't flow!

What you have and what you look like dominates the online dating space, and I didn't want to subscribe to that because those are the last two things on the list of what you really need from your partner. Which is why I feel these types of apps don't help to find long-lasting love. So far, I haven't truly found an app that wasn't focused on looks, so I pulled all of my attention out of dating on apps.

In the end, the person I am with I met in real life on a happenchance occasion. And funnily, I did not even consider her "my type" when we first met! But meeting in person, starting a simple platonic relationship, and letting that grow organically into something more is why I firmly believe meeting people out in a social setting reigns superior to dating apps because dating apps are not real.

Now let's take a look at a quite typical scenario on how two people meet and fall in love.

You meet a good-looking girl at a bar. You ask what she does, and her reply about her profession makes sense to you. From there, the conversation gets a little deeper and you start

asking questions about possible shared interests: skiing, music, art. You start laughing together. You get her number, and the two of you start dating. After a couple dates, you talk about your belief system—whether it's God/Reincarnation/Agnostic. Even further down the road, you talk about family and kids and agree on all these points. One or two years have passed, and now you start thinking out a plan to put your lives together. This process is very natural and real, and it works.

Though it hasn't really been codified, I would say that the way we look at a relationship looks a little like this:

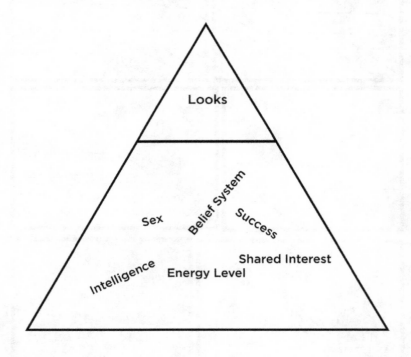

See how everything after how she looks can be a little bit of a confusion? You grab LOOKS first and then throw in everything else you want into a relationship at random as you go. You don't calculate beforehand the important traits—you "find them out." This is where unhappy relationships, constant fights, and other incongruities happen in relationships. Of course, some people may have organized this a little bit more than others, but most keep looks as THE most important and primary thing to pay attention to. I believe the hierarchy of importance in a relationship should look like this:

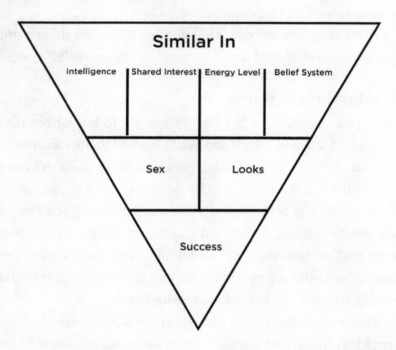

See, after a long relationship, some of the things about a person that you initially thought were essential traits start to become less important, such as looks. After you fall in love with someone, how they look becomes a very small part of what you need from them. Yes, it does help to keep sex flourishing by creating intimacies that lead to sex, such as rubbing someone's shoulders when they are typing at the computer, spanking each other in the kitchen, complimenting each other, taking care of your appearance for the other, offering to get someone something to eat, stroking each other's bodies, and so on. But sex, though important, is not what keeps the relationship together. A relationship is superimposed on LIFE, which includes work, problems, challenges, goals, aging, etc., so a relationship has to be seen as a unified force and team.

What keeps a relationship together are these four things: similar intelligence, shared interest, energy level, and belief system.

Similar Intelligence

Since you can't meet a girl and go straight to testing her IQ, I have found ways in which you could assess whether the two of you are on the same page intelligence-wise. This doesn't mean you both have the same affinity or ability to, say, do mental math, or that you both know all video game trivia since 1982. It just means that you understand each other and can talk to each other without too many miscommunications due to misunderstandings. Also, keep in mind, you want someone at your similar intelligence, not too much lower **or higher**.

One way to test if you two are in the same arena of intelligence is seeing if you two think at the same speed. Simple litmus test: If I ask you a question, how long does it take you to answer, and is that speed the same as mine?

An example of this would be if I ask you how your day was. And a couple of seconds pass by before you answer, but when you ask me, I answer right away. This added time before communication is passed back to you can be quite telling on how intelligent and/or not intelligent someone is. It also gives you an idea on how in present time someone is at that moment. You ever talked to a stoner? It might take a minute before you get a straight answer from them. Now, there are a lot of geniuses who talk very slowly as well. I would say they might not be in present time like you would imagine. A lot of really smart people and creators are constantly in their own head, so their attention to the outside world isn't high. I am not saying this is good or bad. All I am saying is:

**You need to find someone who shares
the same rate/speed of communication as YOU.**

You need to really take your time to test and understand this. Give it a couple of months to come up with an average median with which to check whether she is returning your communication at the same rate or speed as you are to her. This could seem a little funny at first, but let me illustrate.

Have you ever met a person who, the moment you opened your mouth with a question, they took off like a motormouth and wouldn't stop talking? Or have you ever met a person who talks too fast and is hard to understand? Or, conversely, someone who talks so slow you are like "just spit it out already!" All these are differences in communication speed and, in friendships, they are tolerable and sometimes even quirky and likeable but, in relationships, once the walls are down and the chase is over, you are going to get super annoyed because you will want to have a back and forth with your girl without so much added time in between.

You don't have to take my word for it, but if you haven't already experienced this, when you do, you will understand what I mean. You want your communication speed to be the same. Your communications should flow. Conversations with your significant other should be easy to have and fluid. You shouldn't have to repeat yourself a hundred times to get a point across. Or she shouldn't be talking to the point where you start gazing off in the distance while she is still talking.

If there is a disparity here, one person will always be waiting for a return answer, and the other person will always feel rushed. Or one person is always talking and the other one is always listening. This doesn't work for either side. Because nobody wants to feel like they are dragging somebody all the time and, conversely, nobody wants to get dragged either. In time, this difference will be noticed, and it's not a pretty outcome. It frustrates both sides.

Shared Interests

Shared interests can be anything you two agree on, like activities you both like. Maybe you both like art, maybe you both like flying in private jets and traveling, maybe you both like sitting at home and watching TV. Maybe you like the same type of comedy/music. Maybe you have the same group of friends. Maybe you grew up in the same town and so share that reality about that lifestyle/hardship.

I'll give you an example where (not having) shared interest really made a relationship go wrong. I am a very extroverted type of person, and I always love to meet new people. I used to always think I wanted someone opposite of me. I don't think this is a good idea at all anymore. The "opposites attract" idea comes from electronics/physics, not from actual relationships working on the basis that the people are opposites. But in the past I used to believe this, so I would always date more timid, shy girls. My thought was that it balanced me. And the saying "opposites attract" is a true statement but what they didn't tell you is **opposites don't last**. You need someone to lift your energy up—energy feeding on top of energy, not energy cutting energy to make a balance. When you have two people together where the energy outflow doesn't match, one person will get overwhelmed while the other person gets drained. Let me illustrate.

I would go out with my girlfriend and we would have a pretty good time, but I would do all the introductions and meet all of the people and then introduce her. I was always the one initiating with others. This actually introverted her some more, and she became uninterested in meeting new people altogether because she wasn't actually doing anything—she was just a tag-along. Then pretty soon she wouldn't come to the events at all. Finally, I found myself always going out by myself. And it is truly no fun if you can't share your good times with your significant other. It actually put a damper on me going out as well because I felt I was leaving her alone, and I felt alone without her with me, so neither one of us won.

Conversely, when I realized I wanted to meet someone more similar in their interests as me, I met an extroverted girl. Now, when I go out and start meeting people, I found that she too was meeting people, so we end up meeting more people than before and having more fun! Or if I was in a conversation, she would gladly join in and add to the convo. This is shared interest **adding** to your life—not "balancing" it. That is a key point:

> **Your girl should ADD to your life,**
> **not force you to back-track or withdraw.**

Shared interest is anything you two have learned separately, or together, that you love to do and talk about. Shared interests can be obvious, such as both of you are scuba instructors, trainers, or doctors. Or shared interests can be that you both like to start new projects/businesses. Shared interests are mostly activities rather than thoughts about life, as thoughts about life fit under Belief System. Just know that if you don't share enough interests between each other, you will lack the foundation you need to keep wanting to do things together, and, in the long term, your relationship will crash because you need this!

Energy Level

This is a huge one. You can look at this as production level, will and drive. If you are the type of person who is go-go-go, and your girlfriend isn't, in time this difference can be exasperating for both of you! Or if you are the type who is chill and all she wants to do is go-go-go, it also doesn't work because when you want to watch a movie and chill, she wants to party or work, ALL THE TIME! Energy could be one of those things you were born with or it could be learned, but when you don't share the same energy/ production level as your partner, this will become a problem. Production level means the amount of things you do. You could be in five clubs, working, working out, taking care of your dog, parents, and volunteering, while your significant other might just want to sit at home and wait for the phone to ring from an agent. There are many different scenarios here, but energy/production/will/drive (EPWD) is something you will notice, and if you don't feel you two have the same EPWD... keep it moving.

Not having a similar EPWD does not work. One person is working all day while the other is sitting around waiting for the world to bestow them with some magic. And the guy or girl stays in the relationship because they have some false idea that this might change. People are people, the amount they will change their basic character is quite small. Tons of things can change around them—new job, plastic surgery, getting in shape—but basic personality will 99 out of 100 times be the same. I'll share with you a secret to finding this basic personality faster.

People will revert back to their regular selves after a few months of dating. In the beginning, social veneer masks their true nature. When you first meet them, it is like meeting their representative/their PR agent. They are all chipper and doing all the things you love to do. They are eating healthy, maybe even going to the gym, they aren't doing any drugs, and they are typically energetic. A few months pass and they become less active, pick up that drug habit again, start eating like shit. Don't be fooled by the beginnings of a relationship. It is a science. If you are high in energy by nature, anything that gets around you will have to speed up.

A great example is when two people are walking. If one person walks faster than the other they will both have to alter their pace to walk together. So, let's say you walk fast but your partner doesn't. In the beginning, they will appease you and walk fast, and you might even walk a little slower to appease her as well. But when time passes, the person's necessity to stay in this tweaked energy level will fade because they got you now, and they will go back to who they really are—a slow walker! And you will go back to who you are—a fast walker! This is why I always say give your relationships some time before you just go jumping in. Time tells all, don't fall for the social veneer, do your due diligence and take your time before you start planning your future with a girl. This is your life partner we are talking about here.

Energy level, production level, will and drive all fit under this one area of energy level. Don't be a fool and miss this point ever, because you will pay dearly later in a lost relationship and a broken heart. For all you men out there who get googly-eyed by a beautiful girl, don't make excuses for her just because she is "hot." Hot will fade in time, it's just true, and you are left with what you are left with. No human being escapes aging and if you are thinking life partner, then think without your you-know-what on this one, because your you-know-what won't save you from a broken heart and wasted time.

Belief System

This may seem like religion, but this isn't what I am talking about. In fact, there are many people who marry out of their religion. This isn't what religion you were raised in, or even how you were raised per se. It is what you believe about life now, how you live it, and why you live it that way.

Times have changed, and according to a Pew Research Center study, the amount of people who look outside of their religion and culture for suitable partners has increased[17]. We, as a people, have grown quite a bit more tolerant and accepting of others because of the web and social media. This sharing of information has given us insight on both religion and race. If you want to see why people may loathe a group or race, you can look it up. If you want to hear what that group/race says in their defense, you can google it.

So, a belief system is not your religion, it is what you believe now. For instance, being a Christian, even though they believe in God, doesn't mean they wait for God to give them something and that only God will give them grace. There are those Christians who know they need to go out and get it. Or being a Buddhist, though not explicit believers in God, doesn't mean they don't believe in having faith and believing in something.

Belief system is about how you operate your life and your tenants of operating and handling life. Is it okay to yell at each other if you're fighting? Do you believe in yelling at all? How do we handle each other in a discourse? Do you want to take a break and breathe it out and return to it later? Do you want to make sure you never go to sleep on an argument? Do you agree on how to raise kids? Do you agree on having kids? Do you agree on what is healthy? Do you care about being healthy? Do you agree on helping people? Do you want to help people? Do you both just want to be rich? Do you want to live in the boondocks? These are your beliefs, and if they don't line up with your significant other, that relationship won't last long, or if you force it to last, you'll be in contest with her constantly and, thus, unhappy.

---

17   Murphy, Caryle. "Interfaith Marriage Is Common in U.S., Particularly among the Recently Wed." Pew Research Center, June 2, 2015. https://www.pewresearch. org/fact-tank/2015/06/02/interfaith-marriage/.

Your core beliefs on how you live your life are yours to have and the likelihood of you changing them for someone else is low because you feel very strongly about them. They are the motor you put gas in every day. They are your foundation when you build a house. I'll give an example to illustrate.

If I don't believe in hitting kids as a form of discipline then I would never be okay with my wife doing it. Or if I didn't believe in drugs, then a relationship with a druggie won't last long. If I didn't want kids and my girl did, we would eventually break up. If I wanted to be famous and my girl wasn't interested in being in the limelight, she would be counter-intending my success, which would also end in a breakup. Core beliefs are ones you **don't** change because you feel so strongly about them.

Now, there is always compromise in every relationship. But the compromise can't go against your core beliefs because you will find, at some point, that you will rescind this compromise, which will cause more problems later. For example, if you want to have kids and your girl doesn't, this will ultimately kill you inside as you yearn for a family and she just doesn't care for having one. Belief system is an important facet of a long-lasting relationship, and just to be clear: This isn't usually good for a first date/outing conversation. Nevertheless, it's one you will need to have!

The Rest of the Traits

When these four things—intelligence, shared interest, energy level, and belief system—match up well, it will create a long-lasting relationship. In fact, it creates a great friendship! Now add looks and sex to this friendship, and damn—it's a party!! Looks are important, as we mentioned before, as it makes for a constant attraction and does the job of getting you to the physical space of the woman and keeping you there.

Sex is abundantly important as well because a healthy sex life keeps you and your partner intimate. Intimacy is super important in a relationship as it satisfies that urge for closeness every man and woman has. If you two are having bad sex, it should be discussed and hashed out. If you can't get on the same page in the bedroom, this is also a deal breaker. Because sexual desire is a huge part of life, if it isn't met, then you will suffer in the long run. Sex is an activity and, like any activity, the more you do it and talk about it, the better it will get for the both of you!

This leaves us with success at the bottom of the list! Dang. Oh, how far hath success been driven down. Well, not to say success isn't important as it is the basis of survival, but when two people are great friends, the thing they do the most for each other is support each other! They support each other's dreams and help each other reach their goals. If you have the first four things on the first tier—intelligence, shared interest, shared energy level, belief system—and the second two things on the second tier—looks and sex—you and your girl will find success together! This will happen. I have seen it. I have lived it.

Well, now you have it all! Now it is time to go out and have fun! Know what you are looking for—someone who shares similar intelligence, interests, energy, and beliefs as you—and you won't get nervous meeting anyone because if you don't share it, then staying in communication with that person won't matter to you. The one who shines and talks to you and can relate to you will be "the one." Beauty is in the eye of the beholder, my friend. Have you ever noticed the more you have in common with someone, the more you like them? Have you ever talked to someone and you didn't think he/she was that cute, but after having an amazing conversation, you are totally enamored by that person? That is because when you have so many shared interests, you want to talk more, and the more you talk, the higher affinity you have for someone, and these are the makings of a love relationship.

This does happen; it is real. So have fun when you are out and meet people! And when you are looking for a "girl," find what matters in a girlfriend—not what you have been inculcated to believe. TV/Film sensationalize things; it isn't real. Don't be that fool who buys into it. It isn't real. I have worked on films where they have thrown me over a table and I broke it with my back. That wasn't real; the table was precut and I was wearing pads. I have played the love interest with a girl. When we kiss, we don't use tongue, and it is not sensual. It is acting! These things you see aren't real. Nobody is an Instagram model. They take pictures with the right light and a staged environment to capture a moment in time that they themselves also can't hold on to. Why do you think Instagram has filters?

The real you is right in front of you, embrace that, and put the focus there. The women you meet every day out in the world; they are real. Remember, what you focus on grows, so focus on what you can see with your own eyes and the people you meet in person. And remember your significant other constitutes only one piece of the pie. You have you, your work, your family, your friends, the human race, your pets, and all other living things, the universe and beyond to look forward to being a part of.

A genuine nature is just that. We have all been given a bunch of false information on girls: finding them, talking to them, getting with them, loving them, marrying them. I've found the information out there to really confuse me, so I wanted to give you some basics I've learned on the subject. I hope this has helped shed some light on the subject. Humans are social creatures and as social creatures, if we lose our ability to be social because of "the pressures" we feel from the outside world making us not communicate with our fellow man, then we have lost an integral part of who we are. Also, relying on technology to be the sole channel of communication is missing out on real life because people can fake it there, but they can't when they are right in front of you because being out in front of people takes courage and confidence.

So, we have now finished all the steps. What you should be intending when you meet people. Your Intention. How you should be sensitive to what they are going through at the moment by Watch and Learn. How to not be a stalker by Touch and Go. We have also talked about your group and all the possible scenarios of groups from Loners to Straggler to Groupers. Now you know why you should Diversify Your Risk and how that dovetails into Building a Network. And lastly, you know what you should be looking for. Shoot, you have it all!

Now, go out and meet people! Be the best you, the most genuine you. See the room, hall, school playground for what it is: a bunch of people trying to find their place in the world. Let yourself fly free into that space. Look for those who seem friendly and want to talk to you, use the steps I've explained here, open up the room and make your moves, always knowing there can be no fear of rejection if there are no expectations. Always knowing that if a person is rude to you, then that is their loss. Always knowing that what you bring to the table in any conversation is love and your true self, and that is valuable! With these thoughts in mind, I am sure you will win!

Now get out there and do it! I believe in you.

Bonus Chapter

PROOF YOU CAN CHANGE INTO WHO YOU WANT TO BE

O ne of the most important things we need to realize is that we can change. Naturally, you know many people who haven't changed, so it's easy to adopt this idea that "people don't change." But when faced with a life that's less than great, you know you have to change. And that's when you do.

People change when they *have* to.

Sometimes that "have to" comes in the form of "I want to change so badly!" but nevertheless, it's a "have to change" scenario. I would argue that ONLY when you've arrived at "I *have* to change" will you, in fact, change. Otherwise, you become another person who tries a new habit, but fails to make it stick… and you, and your life, both stay the same.

I wanted to share my story of how I changed from the BIG-GEST loser with girls and a general social outcast to someone who can comfortably communicate with anyone, women included. And I also want to prove to you that no matter where you come from, what you look like, and where you're starting on your journey with women, you can make a change in you and your life.

I grew up in a small suburban town outside Los Angeles called South Pasadena. Though Los Angeles itself is obviously a massive city, South Pasadena resides on the fringes of L.A. with a total population of 25,000. So, I'm from L.A., but most of where I grew up was in this small community.

My dad single-handedly immigrated not only himself, but many of his fellow countrymen and relatives to America from Sri Lanka before I was born. This is no small move, by the way… Here's Sri Lanka:

As an immigrant who literally started out as a minority with $0 in a brand-new country, my dad demanded my siblings and I receive an incredible education. For immigrant families like ours, job security is all we have to make sure we survive, and job security starts out with education.

I started school at a nearby private school, which was incredibly small. In fact, there were only 11 people in my entire grade, and that included me! I grew up with these same 10 people all the way from kindergarten up through fifth grade. These classmates became my second family. I saw the girls and boys as completely the same. I never conceived of viewing girls as anything different or sexual because they were basically like sisters to me.

In sixth grade, I transferred from that tiny private school to a large public school in the neighboring city. Now my class had 250 students (twenty-two times bigger)! That's when my social life turned on its head and became cuckoo crazy. I tried to make new friends, and I was outright shunned, but I couldn't figure out why. The only reason I could see was that I was the only dark-skinned kid in my grade (out of 250 students), while everyone else was either White or Asian. But an additional truth was that I was terribly awkward, and I was the new kid in town.

This new school environment quickly enlightened me on this idea that girls equal a new kind of excitement for boys—an ideology I was never exposed to in my previous school. For example, at my previous school, we wore boring uniforms, so I never even noticed the "girl parts" that were *clearly* put on display at the new public school. Like other boys, I quickly realized that all those bare legs and low-cut shirts did things to my pubescent body that had never happened before.

On top of physically seeing girls' bodies for the first time, my guy friends started giving me these false ideas that girls are different and "should be treated differently." These ideas seeped into my mind, and before I had a chance to introduce myself to any of the girls to simply try and make friends, I began putting them on the proverbial pedestal—separating them from me in my mind.

This separation between boys and girls made me even more introverted and nervous, and I found it very hard to communicate with them, literally fumbling on what to say. I started believing my friends that conversation with girls had to be pre-planned like a military strategy before I could just candidly walk up and talk to them.

**I became afraid that girls wouldn't like me,
and if they didn't like me, I wouldn't be "cool."**

Stack those worries on top of my puberty-plagued body, and I was a walking stress ball (with a hint of curry). Plus, with 250 students in your grade, there were tons of cliques: the cool girls, the stoner girls, the sluts, nerdy girls, etc. These new social groups seemed crazy to me! Snack break and lunchtime would come and everyone would "clique up," leaving me holding my lunch tray while standing in the middle of the cafeteria wondering what to do with myself.

After lunch, the girls would congregate outside chatting amongst themselves. You might as well have put a velvet rope around them with a sign that said "VIP section." There was literally no way to approach them, and if I wanted to talk to one

girl, I would have to approach the whole group of girls. As if it wasn't already hard to meet just one! I had to approach all of them, staring at me and talking amongst themselves about my every move. It was miserable!

I didn't know the first thing about communicating with girls in this new environment because I had listened to my friends' advice that overtly separated girls from boys, which made girls very intimidating.

I needed help navigating this social landscape but didn't have anyone to turn to. My parents were straight-up foreigners with VERY thick immigrant accents. It's as if physically they lived in America, but mentally and culturally, they still were in Sri Lanka. The help I did get from my dad on the subject of girls boiled down to sex and was basically the equivalent of a public health poster. His sole sage advice?

"Use a condom."

"Dad, I am not having sex," I replied. "I'm in sixth grade."

"I don't care, just use a condom."

And that was it.

Here's some more bad advice I unwittingly accepted from my friends at school:

"You need to act tough." "Girls like bad boys."

Any of that sound familiar?

Desperate to fit into this new school (remember, I'm still the new and ONLY brown kid on the block with no friends, AND I'm going through puberty), I thought, "Well, if girls like bad boys, I can try and do that!" So, I tried to emulate the "bad boy facade," and this approach resulted in me showing off during lunch playing basketball in front of the girls. Maybe they would notice me now? Psst, yeah right!

In sixth grade, I got suspended three separate times, and almost got expelled for fighting and various other nefarious activities. And the girls did not like me anymore because of it.

My social outcast status hit an all-time high when I decided to ask a girl about a party I heard about, just to see if I asked about it, I would get invited. I walked up to a girl I knew and asked about the party, and she outright said no. Minutes later, I saw her talking to her friends, laughing while directly pointing at me. How humiliating.

I felt like I was losing no matter where I turned. I didn't fit into any of the White, Asian, or other groups. I had no workable guidance on how to be accepted by girls, and I was pimply, scrawny, and visibly different and awkward.

This is where I hit my "tipping point" (shout out to Malcolm Gladwell for an awesome book!). Basically, I quit trying.

I stopped attempting to impress or even talk to anyone else anymore.

Instead, I focused on school and basketball—that's it. I was going back to being who I used to be in fifth grade: a happy, fun, talkative, nice guy. I was going to be me! No more fighting with people, no more showing off.

Now that I swore off people, I had to decide what to do at lunch to get away from the madness of sitting in the cafeteria. Lunchtime is notoriously a social affair about who sits with who, and where. So, at lunch, when the social groups would convene in their regular spots outside and inside the cafeteria, I found a place to sit next to the track that was very far away from everyone so I could eat in peace.

There were a couple of steps leading up to the gym, which was located across from the outside eating area for the cafeteria, and I would sit on those steps alone and eat my very botched ham sandwich. I was far enough away from the cafeteria area to not hear anyone from across the quad, but because I was sitting on those gym steps, I could see everyone and just enjoy my lunch alone—no drama.

I just didn't care anymore. I was happy on my own because I felt like I could be myself. I was free from the pressures of needing to fit in! I could've gone on for the duration of my middle school "career" this way until…

One of the girls who had a class with me came up to me one day and asked me, "Why do you always sit here by yourself?" I told her I enjoyed watching people. Obviously, the reason why I was sitting by myself was that I was just done with people, but I didn't say that. She seemed to find the concept of a middle schooler people-watching fascinating, so she asked to sit with me and I said yes.

I wasn't interested in her in any way other than a friend, and I wasn't thinking of her being a "girl" at that moment at all. She knew me because we had classes together, and since I had reached that point where I didn't care to be anyone else but myself, we began to just talk, just as friends. And after a couple weeks, she and I really did become good friends.

No pretenses, no need for the "extras" like my body having to be sexy or me needing to be some super cool basketball player.

We were just friends. The conversations were real—about family, school, studying, and life. She felt genuinely comfortable with me. She didn't feel threatened as if I wanted something from her, and she was happy just sitting and talking. This went on for about a month. Then she asked me if she could invite one of her friends to come sit with us because she thought I was a really nice guy. I agreed, and now there were three of us.

We all became friends, and before I knew it, each girl had invited another friend, who had invited another friend, and so on. Soon, there were 12 girls sitting with me every day at lunchtime. But we were all *just* friends. We would laugh and talk, and I loved it, and so did they! Somehow without me noticing it, I gradually became this guy who "knew all the girls" at school. This is when the "cool" kids became curious:

"Who is this one guy sitting with 12 girls by himself?"

Then just like that, the "cool" girls—the same ones who didn't want to invite me to parties—wanted to come sit and hang out in this new hangout spot I created. I, of course, said yes and got to know everyone. Not sure if you know this, but when it comes to being cool for the guys, it has everything to do with having access to the girls. So, from there, the "cool" guys came over from the other side of the quad to come sit in this little area I had created.

And after forging all these friendships, in one year, I went from not knowing anyone and not getting invited anywhere to knowing tons of people and always being included in fun parties and get-togethers. For a lack of a better word and totally unintentionally, this once scrawny, pimply, curry-lunch-carrying kid became "cool."

I did not know it at the time, but I was applying all the steps I ended up writing in this book.

And the best part of this story isn't that I got to be "cool" per se:

It was that I completely changed my predicament.

You, too, can completely change your life by first getting some perspective on your situation, also known as confronting who and where and what you are.

Even if you've tried and failed and tried and failed again at something does not mean you can't try again, persist, and meet your goal. But what failing repeatedly may tell you is that you're operating off of bad information. Information that when applied does not factually work for you.

If you're continually unhappy in your career line, maybe you are truly not in the right industry or work type for you.

If you cannot lose weight or bulk up, maybe you are not applying information suited to your body.

If you keep meeting the wrong girls, maybe you are operating off a wrong concept of what kind of girl would be a great partner in your life.

Then, of course, there is the subject of persisting. When you do have the right type of information, you need to persist until you meet your goal. You may be surprised at how much you have to persist to get where you want, but if you persist, you WILL make it there (again, assuming you are operating off of correct information!).

Remember: Don't let anyone tell you that you cannot change. You can change your life, no matter where you're starting out from, what you look like, where you are from and, most importantly, what others have told you about yourself.

Get a firm grip on your own life and take control into your own hands. You can do it. I believe in you!

Dilan Jay

ABOUT THE AUTHOR

D ilan Jay has crammed five lives into one as a writer, musician, actor, filmmaker, and renegade voice for the under-represented. His parents immigrated from Sri Lanka to America before he was born, making his upbringing a cultural cocktail of traditional spiritualism, chicken curry, and urban Los Angeles. He fights for his beliefs, faces off injustice, and aims to light a fire under anyone who thinks they can't achieve their dreams due to color, creed, or culture. Learn more at www.dilanjay.com.

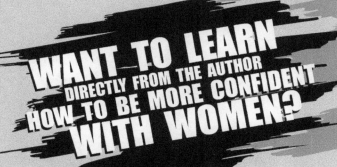

CPSIA information can be obtained
at www.ICGtesting.com
Printed in the USA
JSHW040144080521
14526JS00001B/99

9 781631 953095